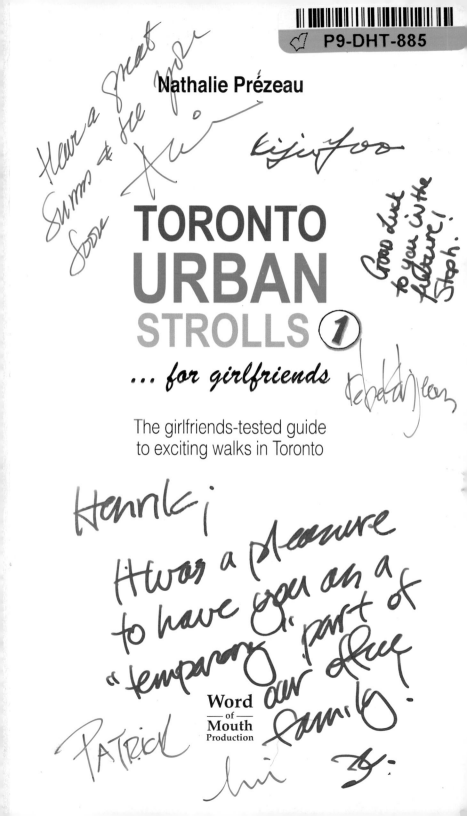

Nathalie Prézeau

TORONTO
URBAN
STROLLS ①

... for girlfriends

The girlfriends-tested guide
to exciting walks in Toronto

Word
— of —
Mouth
Production

This book is dedicated to my mothers' group.
"A friend is one who knows you and loves you just the same."
– Elbert Hubbard

Published by Word-of-Mouth Production
299 Booth Avenue
Toronto, Ontario M4M 2M7, Canada
Tel.: (416) 462-0670
mail@torontofunplaces.com

www.torontofunplaces.com
www.torontourbanstrolls.com

Writing and photos: **Nathalie Prézeau**
Illustrations: **Johanne Pepin**
Proofreading: **Kerstin McCutcheon**
Honorary members of the author's exclusive Friends Whom I Exploit Shamelessly Club:
François Bergeron, Christian Castel, Pascale Chapdelaine, Claire Marier, Julie Sabourin

Design and layout: **Publisher Friendly Inc.** (416) 462-0459
Printing: **Marquis Book Printing Inc.** (418) 246-5666

Library and Archives Canada Cataloguing in Publication

Prézeau, Nathalie, 1960 –
   Toronto urban strolls 1: –for girlfriends : the girlfriends-tested guide to exciting walks
   in Toronto / Nathalie Prézeau. – 2nd ed.

Includes index.
ISBN 978-0-9684432-7-9

1. Toronto (Ont.) – Tours.
2. Walking – Ontario – Toronto – Guidebooks. I. Title. II. Title: Toronto urban strolls one.

FC3097.18.P75 2013   917.13'541045   C2013-901683-X

A word from the author

I'm so glad this book found you!

Last summer, when I wrote and published the first edition of **Toronto Urban Strolls... for girlfriends 1**, I knew I was on to something fun and useful to get us out of the house, but I did not imagine my 5,000 copies would sell out in three months.

Neither did I expect to make the *Globe and Mail*'s bestsellers list!

This new edition offers an updated version of the 28 strolls described in the first edition. It also features a double-page map showing you how the 28 walks are spread around Toronto.

Many carless readers told me they'd like to have more public transportation tips. I heard you! In my information box, I've included the number of TTC's main line and/or subway stations serving each stroll.

Finally, I thought this would be a good place to mention that once you're done with the strolls presented in this guide, there are 24 more walks waiting for you in **Toronto Urban Strolls... for girlfriends 2**. (But hey! No rush! Let's do the strolls one at a time, shall we?)

My TOP-3 reasons for loving to walk?
It is the best way to discover a city. It's the most fun way to stay in shape. And I know from experience that great walks in good company lead to great talks.

Enjoy!

Nathalie Prézeau
Author, publisher, photographer
mail@torontofunplaces.com

TORONTO URBAN STROLLS MAP

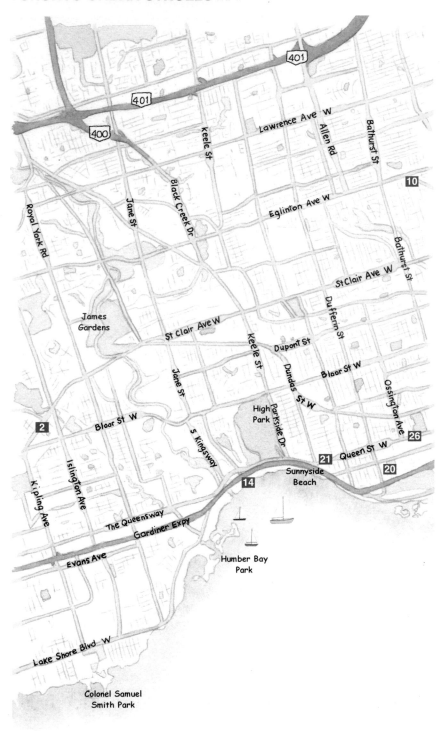

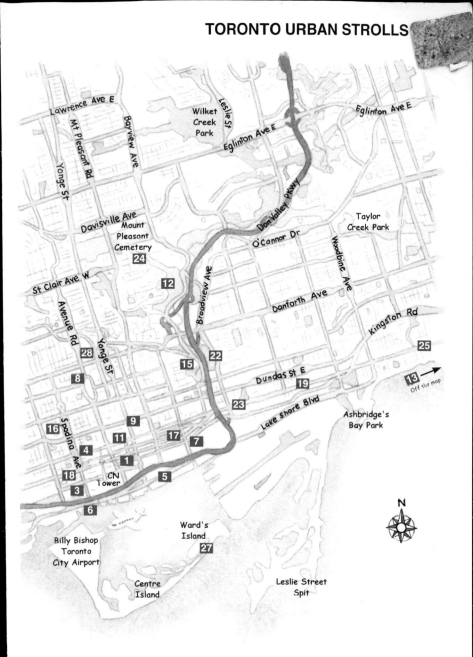

Legend:

1 to 28 = Reference to stroll number in the guide

Table of Contents

I SPY
STROLLS

NATURE
STROLLS

NEIGHBOURHOOD STROLLS

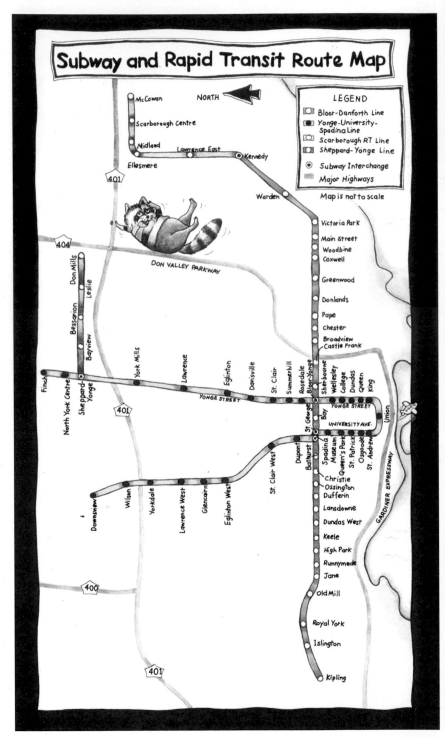

Strolls by subway stations

Want to go carless? Here's a list of Toronto subway stations included in the strolls featured in this guide.

Bay
Included in **Stroll 28**

Broadview
Included in **Stroll 22**

Castle Frank
10-min walk from **Stroll 15**

Davisville
Included in **Stroll 10**

Dundas
Included in **Stroll 9**

Eglinton West
7-min from **Stroll 10**

Islington
10-min walk from **Stroll 2**

King
Included in **Stroll 1**,
7-min walk from **Stroll 17**

Museum
Included in **Stroll 8**

Osgoode
3-min walk from **Stroll 4**,
included in **Stroll 11**

Queen
Included in **Stroll 9**

Queen's Park
Included in **Stroll 8**

St. Andrew
Included in **Stroll 1**

St. Patrick
3-min walk from **Stroll 4**

Union
Included in **Stroll 1**,
3-min walk from **Stroll 3**,
10-min walk from **Stroll 5**
and **Stroll 6**,
5-min walk from **Stroll 7**

Spectacular *Cross Section* by **William McElcheran** (northwest entrance to Dundas Station).

Shiny enamel mural *Tempo* by **Gordon Rayner** (mezzanine level in St. Clair West Station).

There's **24 more** themed walks in **Toronto Urban Strolls** 2

Did you really think the author would have left out Danforth, Forest Hill, The Junction, Ossington and the likes? No way!

(Photo from Stroll 16: **Waterfalls Indian Tapas**)

That's the life!

Spending time with friends on a patio is so relaxing, it truly feels like a holiday. In the summer, the cool cocktail looks prettier under the sun. In the fall, the warm coffee feels better between our hands. (It's a good thing that many places stretch the season with patio heaters.)

(Photo from Stroll 7: **The Distillery**)

Why so serious?

When you feel overstretched and life is reduced to a to-do list, it means it's time to go out with your girlfriends. Have you noticed how they bring the funniest version of your-self? It only takes a couple of hours for friendship to work its magic.

DOWNTOWN
COURTYARDS STROLL
1

Finding high-rise blocks cold?

Maybe it's because you never think to look down when you're near skyscrapers. Or maybe you've only driven by them but never had a chance to check out what they're hiding from the street. Look carefully, and you'll realize that this "boring" downtown is actually full of surprising courtyards, most of them within view of one another. As you play the tourist and hop from one courtyard to the next, this stroll is sure to remind you that we are indeed in Canada's biggest and richest city. Stop for coffee at one of the downtown patios to truly feel the urban vibe of Toronto.

STROLL 1

Full loop:
4.6 km (1 hr 10 min)

Shorter version:
The best urban sights are found along the 2.3 km section of **Stroll 1**, east of Bay Street. Park in the indoor lot at the foot of Church, then start the stroll at Front Street.

Game for more?
The **Yonge Street Hidden Treasures Stroll** (**Stroll 9**, p. 55) includes Queen Street, one block north of **Cloud Gardens**.

Parking & TTC
• Exit at **St. Andrews**, **Union** or **King Subway Stations**.
• The parking lot under **Scotiabank Theatre** (entrances off Richmond and John Streets) is the easiest option.
• At the foot of Church Street is an affordable indoor parking lot.

Other TIPS
• A good finish to this stroll would be a matinee at **TIFF Bell Lightbox**. Check www.tiff.net for their listing of great movies you will see nowhere else.

Roy Thomson Hall
Breakfast or lunch at **O & B Canteen** in **TIFF Bell Lightbox** is a great way to start (opens daily at 8 a.m.). Chic **Luma** and the slick lounge, both on the **Lightbox**'s 2nd floor, offer fancier lunch options on weekdays.

Walk east on King and enter **Metro Hall** (before the large plaza by **Roy Thomson Hall**).

1 See how the sparkling metal mixes with the floor to ceiling glass walls. It feels like a futuristic cathedral.

2 Don't miss the big shiny arrow. Doesn't it look like a giant "You are here" mark on a map? Go back into the plaza now called **David Pecaut Square** to admire the great fountain.

3 Look down at the foot of **Roy Thomson** along King Street, to view the surprisingly large pond you could not see from the street.

4 **St. Andrews Church** is next. You should enter to have a look at what elegant Romanesque architecture looks like, with a unique round upper gallery and gorgeous stained glass windows.

Toronto Dominion
5 Turn right on the east side of York, through the corridor just before **Toronto Dominion Centre**, to access the courtyard. See the cows? They're the creation of Joe Fafard. Cows in the middle of the financial district's rat race. Hilarious, isn't it?

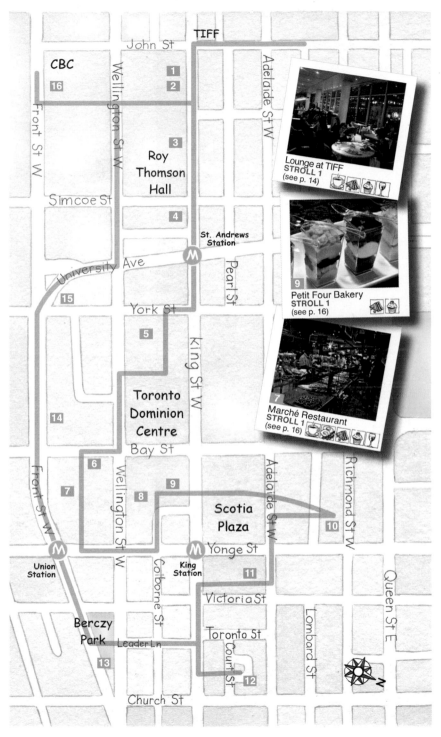

Lounge at TIFF
STROLL 1
(see p. 14)

Petit Four Bakery
STROLL 1
(see p. 16)

Marché Restaurant
STROLL 1
(see p. 16)

6 Go left on Wellington, cross Bay Street and turn right to the entrance to **Brookfield Place**. Before entering, look up to see a special urban landscape. Once inside, check the glasswork by **Ki**'s entrance (the restaurant on your left).

Brookfield Place

7 The great arches of the glass ceiling, juxtaposed with the heritage facade (from the 1890's-era on Wellington Street) is a perfect example of a great integration of old and new architecture.

Weather permitting, the **Marché Restaurant** opens a beautiful outdoor patio on the south side of **Brookfield Place**.

Commerce Court

8 Exit on Yonge and turn left. Turn left again on Melinda St. to access the courtyard of **Commerce Court**. See the elephants?

This is another good spot to look up and feel very small amidst all the skyscrapers. (The panorama becomes a visual feast in gold and blue, when the afternoon sun reflects on the buildings.)

9 For a fun treat, go through the arch and down the stairs by the CIBC to **West Commerce Court**. Straight ahead, you'll find **Petit Four**, selling a selection of the cutest (under $3) desserts served in a tiny cup.

Cross King to enter **Scotia Plaza**, on the north side. (Within the **Scotia Bank** awaits the spectacular painting of a high waterfall.)

Cloud Gardens

Walk north through **Scotia Plaza** to reach Adelaide Street. Some might want to know there is a **Winners** in the building to your right on Adelaide (closed on weekends).

10 Across Adelaide, there's a vast open space from which you can see **Cloud Gardens**. The large artwork gets even more interesting when you learn that each square represents different trades in the construction industry. Also included is a little waterfall, walkways and a greenhouse (with very short hours of operation).

Metropolitan

11 Walk left along Adelaide (past Yonge) and there it is: a chiseled glass labyrinth leading to the lovely courtyard with an assortment of sculptures with fountains.

The **Metropolitan** opens a patio by the sculptures during the summer. It's a great spot for a glass of wine under the sun. (Note that smokers working nearby come to this courtyard for their cigarette break.) The restaurant itself is zen and chic, and opens Monday to Friday at 11:30 a.m.

Court Square

12 South of the courtyard, turn left on King and walk to an alleyway past Toronto Street.

The path leads to a little square with a granite platform and a lovely arch with benches. It is adjacent to the inviting backyard patio of **Terroni** (57 Adelaide East). The perfect hideaway for lunch or drinks!

Front Street

13 Back on King, turn right then left on Leader Lane. Straight ahead, it will lead you to **Berczy Park**. There's an European feel to this park with a fountain and surrounded by old brick buildings. (The mural reproduces the facade of nearby **Winners**.)

Then, it's a long stroll west along Front Street. (**Nicholas Hoare**'s classy bookstore on Front has unfortunately closed.)

14 If you happen to do the stroll on a weekday, go see the fantastic patio of **Royal Bank Plaza** (open weekdays 11:30 a.m. to 5 p.m., closed in the winter). It is up the stairs by the colourful characters on the RBC wall, in front of **Union Station**.

15 Further west, peek inside the **Fairmount Royal York**, then I recommend a stop at the patio of **Second Cup**, west of the hotel to feel the urban vibe.

16 Continue north on University and left at Wellington, to explore the courtyard on your left by **CBC**. Around the building, you'll see the aluminium mountain by Anish Kapoor, the monument to workers, and a life-size Glen Gould on a bench. Then go inside to admire the ceiling.

ISLINGTON VILLAGE
MURALS STROLL

2

Best mural spotting in town

Nobody was going out of their way to visit this stretch of Dundas West so local business and community members came up with a great idea. They found an amazing artist (John Kuna, a graduate of **OCAD**, Toronto) to paint most of the gorgeous murals gracing many walls of what is becoming an outdoor gallery. Gentrification has not reached this part of town yet (which adds to the fun of discovering these gems amidst little unpolished stores and unassuming restaurants) but cute businesses are starting to pop up. You can grab macarons at **European Patisserie** and enjoy one more mural while eating inside the lovely **Village Trattoria**.

STROLL 2

Full loop:
2.4 km (40 min)

Shorter version:
Most of the murals are located along the .5 km stretch on Dundas Street West between Cordoba Avenue and just west of Michael Power Place.

Game for more?
If you go south down the path in the garden by **Montgomery's Inn**, you'll reach the pretty **Thomas Riley Park**. Mimico Creek runs through it and Bloor Street borders it on the other side. This will add 2 km (30 min) to your stroll.

Parking & TTC
• **Islington Subway Station** is a 10-min. walk from **Montgomery's Inn**.
• There's lots of cheap parking space in the alley north of Dundas West, between Royalavon Crescent and Renown Road.

Other TIPS
• Check the website **villageofislington. com** to download their walking tour guide.

Royalavon Crescent

1 The advantage of parking in the alley just west of Royalavon Crescent is that you can start the stroll with a macaron from the **European Patisserie** (5072 Dundas West), which you can eat under the large gazebo in the park across the street.

2 To get your first glimpse of the gorgeous murals of artist John Kuna, walk to 5126 Dundas West. You'll see old fashioned bathers frolicking in Mimico Creek by a sawmill.

Then walk eastbound to enjoy more murals on the north side of Dundas Street.

Avonhurst Road

A new mural with a fishing theme was added at 5096 Dundas West.

3 A music theme one is on the west side of Avonhurst (5048 Dundas W.).

On the east side of it, past the first building, is a truly original painting of a Lancaster Bomber dropping flyers over football players (4994 Dundas W.).

4 A bit further, just around the corner of Cabot Court, you'll see a firetruck by a skating rink.

5 It faces a lovely rendering of a bucolic scene of a painter by the Mimico Creek, during the fall (4986 Dundas W.).

6 Two other monochrome murals of old scenes with interesting details from daily life, are facing each other at 4984 and 4972 Dundas West in a parking lot.

A bit further, by the old cemetery, you'll see a series of old vehicles adorning the facade of the **Seniors' Centre** at 4968 Dundas West.

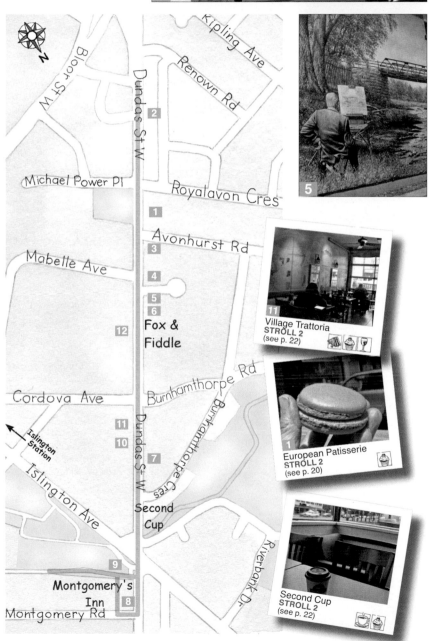

Village Trattoria
STROLL 2
(see p. 22)

European Patisserie
STROLL 2
(see p. 20)

Second Cup
STROLL 2
(see p. 22)

Burnhamthorpe Rd

You'll find the mural of a scene from the Prohibition... on the **Fox & Fiddle Pub** (4946 Dundas W.) and the portrait of a shoe maker by the muralist Sarah Collard at 4884 Dundas West.

The most recent mural features a regiment in the back of **CIBC** (4914 Dundas W.).

7 I caught John Kuna while he was painting the mural further east at 4868 Dundas West!

Islington Avenue

8 From there, it's a 3-min walk to a **Second Cup** or you could walk 5 minutes (crossing south at Islington) to get to the tearoom of **Montgomery's Inn** (4709 Dundas W.). Don't expect anything fancy, but you'll be served by a volunteer in period clothes (2 p.m. to 4:30 p.m., closed Mondays).

9 Go down the stairs in the back of the Inn for a short stroll in the park.

10 On your way back, stay on the south side of Dundas. Past the **Rabba's** store, you'll be able to see through the walls of a Victorian House at 4879 Dundas West.

11 Further west, by the **Village Trattoria** (an inviting little Italian restaurant with a cute mural adorning its indoor walls), is the beautiful mural of a church (4901 Dundas W.).

12 My favourite mural awaits at 4937 Dundas W. (Notice how the artist winks at painter Claude Monet's *Woman with Umbrella*?)

Go big or stay home!

Have you ever noticed large pieces of public art in unexpected places? It's because Toronto condos have been investing one percent of the gross cost of their development in Public Art since 1986 (as required by the City of Toronto under a special policy). The commissioned works have to be publicly accessible, visually and physically. My favourite is the (still) best kept secret, the huge bobbers in **Canoe Landing Park** off Fort York Boulevard, but there's enough public art in the area to make this stroll amidst over-towering condos an intriguing one worth the detour.

STROLL 3

Full loop:
5 km (1 hr 15 min)

Shorter version:
For a 3.25 km walk (50 min) including the most fascinating art, go down Blue Jays Way and turn left on Navy Wharf Court. Then follow **Stroll 3**, on the west side of the **Rogers Centre** (as shown on map).

Game for more?
You can access the **Queens Quay Harbourfront Stroll** (**Stroll 6**, p. 39) in a few minutes, walking towards the lake from most of the north-south streets in **Stroll 3**.

Parking & TTC
• It's a 20-min. walk southbound on Spadina from Queen W.
• The parking lot on the southwest corner of Wellington West and Blue Jays Way is not too pricey for the area.

Other TIPS
• You'll get $3.50 off the indoor parking fee at **Sobeys** (on Fort York Blvd, before **Canoe Landing**) if you make a minimum purchase of $10.

Breakfast anyone?
1 I prefer to park in the parking lot at the corner of Wellington and Blue Jays Way (just a bit off **Stroll 3** map). There's a **Cora's** just across the street (southeast corner of Blue Jays Way and Wellington). My girlfriends and I have enjoyed many meals in this all-day breakfast chain. Most plates are always nicely adorned with colourful fruit. (It closes at 3 p.m. but opens at least at 7 a.m.!)

For a fancier brunch, I've been to chic **Senses** in the **SoHo Hotel** also across from the parking lot, northwest corner of Blue Jays Way and Wellington (at 11:30 a.m. on weekends).

Blue Jays Way
2 **Wayne Gretzky's**, one block north at 99 Blue Jays Way, has the perfect rooftop patio for drinks: **Oasis** (and it's heated until October). It features a little waterfall which adds to the illusion of being in a Fort Lauderdale bar! (Note that **Oasis** offers a limited menu.)

3 Walking south on Blue Jays Way, you'll soon observe the sculpture of giant people leaning over the balcony of the **Rogers Centre**.

4 Following Blue Jays Way, you'll see the huge monument to the Chinese-Canadian railway workers, impressive when you admire it from its base.

5 Around the memorial is a path going east through a tunnel. It leads to

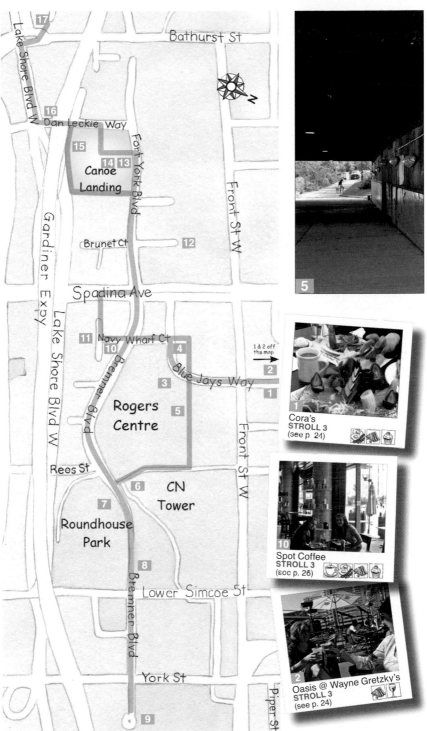

Bathurst St

Lake Shore Blvd W

17

16 Dan Leckie Way

15

Fort York Blvd

14 **13**

Canoe Landing

Front St W

Gardiner Expy

Lake Shore Blvd W

Brunet Ct

12

Spadina Ave

11 Navy Wharf Ct

10

Bremner Blvd

4

3

Blue Jays Way

1 & 2 off the map

2

1

Rogers Centre

5

Reos St

6

Front St W

CN Tower

7

Roundhouse Park

8

Bremner Blvd

Lower Simcoe St

York St

Piper St

9

5

Cora's
STROLL 3
(see p. 24)

10 Spot Coffee
STROLL 3
(see p. 26)

Oasis @ Wayne Gretzky's
STROLL 3
(see p. 24)

the other side of **Rogers Centre**, where more mischievous giants await.

CN Tower

6 After you've looked up for a good view of Toronto's landmark, go down the stairs and you'll see the back of a gorgeous fountain with elegant metal salmon. Walk around for a better view. (Last time I checked, it was dry but they might have filled it since.)

Bremner Boulevard

7 Strolling eastbound, you'll see the new **Roundhouse Park**, with real round table, locomotives and a small track for little train rides. It includes a lovely mural not too far from the entrance to... a **Leon's Furniture** store! (I agree it's an awkward place for such a store but I must say they did a very good job at integrating the new with the old.)

8 Further, to your left, you'll see the two giant woodpeckers on a pole by the **Convention Centre**.

9 At the end of Bremner, a couple of blocks further east, you'll reach the roundabout at the **Air Canada Centre**. It has undergone major renovations in the last years but we can still admire the two huge beams pierced with star-shaped holes.

Navy Wharf Court

10 Walking back west along Bremner Boulevard, past **Rogers Centre**, you'll see the pretty **Spot Coffee**, serving decent coffee, breakfast and light lunch (333 Bremner).

11 Look north on Navy Wharf Court and you'll see the monument to the Chinese workers from afar. Then walk south to see what I think is the most spectacular public art in Toronto: *Barca Volante*, from the Chilean artist Francisco Gazitua.

Completely off the beaten track, the immense steel sculpture gracefully stands over a reflecting pool, which adds to the impression of airy lightness.

Keep walking towards Spadina and across the street, you'll find another sculpture from the same artist. You can't see it from where you stand but it is surrounded by tall grass.

Fort York Boulevard

12 Bremner Boulevard becomes Fort York Boulevard on the west side of Spadina. Walk past the **Sobeys Urban Fresh** grocery store and look north around the corner at Telegraph Mews, for a big red sculpture.

13 Further west on Fort York Boulevard, you'll see the outstanding **Canoe Landing Park** (still towered over by construction cranes at the time of print).

I was in awe of the colourful fishing bobbers standing in front of me by the entrance. They were so whimsical, especially with all the serious buildings and **CN Tower** in the background.

Even better, there's a rubber button on the floor amidst the structures which you can push to activate the water sprays.

I was in the area at night last winter and was surprised to find this secluded public art fully lit, for my sole enjoyment!

14 The fishing floats are the creation of Douglas Coupland (the guy who coined Generation X). He's also responsible for the modern "beaver dam" nearby and the giant red canoe.

15 The red canoe, in the southwest corner of the park, is large enough for drivers to notice from the Gardiner Expressway. Hop in and you will feel like you're about to fly over the highway.

Dan Leckie Way

16 Walking down the stairs to reach Dan Leckie Way, turn left to get under the Gardiner, for another surprising sight of a condo's concrete driveway with a funky twist: spotted columns and swirls painted in blue on the asphalt.

T.O. Tuck Shop, a convenience café, is just around the corner.

Bathurst Street

17 Last but not least, are the giant toy soldiers, also from artist Douglas Coupland. Walk west along Lake Shore to Bathurst Street and you'll see them at the northwest corner of Bathurst and Fleet Streets.

On your way back to **Canoe Landing**, you'll see a path going up, just south of the park. It will take you around the field where you'll see the **Terry Fox Miracle Mile**, a running circuit marked by more intriguing art pieces by Coupland.

So many cool spots to see!

When we stick to Queen Street around John Street (home of **MuchMusic Broadcaster**, **Scotiabank Cinema** and the **CN Tower**), it feels like the retail chains have eaten up part of Queen West's soul. It's easy to miss many of the cool sights that would prove to you that this stretch has not totally surrendered to tourists and young adults looking for entertainment. The artsy vibe prevails (if you know where to look).

STROLL 4

Full loop:
4.2 km (65 min)

Shorter version:
The coolest part of this stroll, the graffiti lane, is in the 1.5 km section of the stroll west of Spadina (a 25 min walk). You'll find cheap parking spaces on Denison, north of Queen.

Game for more?
Trinity-Bellwoods Artsy Stroll (**Stroll 26**, p. 155) also runs along Queen West and starts just west of Bathurst Street.

Parking & TTC
• The streetcar **#501** runs along Queen.
• The parking lot under **Scotiabank Theatre** (entrances off Richmond and John) is the easiest option.

Other TIPS
• Street art is responsible for the urban street vibe of **Stroll 4**. It appears graffiti is an endangered species (some confusing it with tag signatures). The graffiti and mural spots mentioned here still existed at the time of print, but they are ever changing.

John Street
1 If you park around John Street, you'll be in the middle of the mainstream action, with the **Scotiabank Theatre**, across from the fancy bowling alley and restaurant **The Ballroom** and next to an **Indigo**.

2 Aim north on John Street, past Queen Street, and let the street smart fun begin, starting with pink **Umbra** store and its great home accessories and furniture selection.

3 Past that, you'll enter the peaceful oasis of the **Grange Park**, preceded by a beautiful little church and a labyrinth painted on the small plaza.

Amidst the trees, you can see the modern architecture of the **AGO**.

4 Walk east through the park and another modern building will pop out: the **OCAD**. I especially like the view point we get of **OCAD** when standing in front of the great store **Aboveground Arts Supplies** (74 McCaul Street).

McCaul Street
5 A great mural spills over the tiny private parking lot just north of 52 McCaul Street.

On the south side of this building, awaits another fantastic (and huge) mural by the large parking lot.

6 On your way to Queen Street, you might want to check the amazing costume store **Malabar** (14 McCaul Street). This is your chance to model a Shakespearian petticoat for your friends!

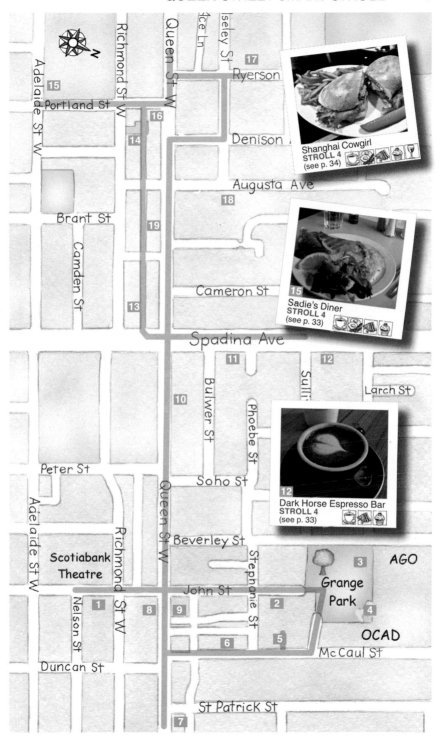

Shanghai Cowgirl
STROLL 4
(see p. 34)

Sadie's Diner
STROLL 4
(see p. 33)

Dark Horse Espresso Bar
STROLL 4
(see p. 33)

Queen West

This is the Street Smart Stroll, remember? Walk one block east of McCaul for a visit to a couple of specialty stores: **Friendly Stranger**, the self-described "cannabis culture shop" (241 Queen West), and the **Condom Shack** (231).

7 Both are located across from the **Rex Hotel**. In addition to their evening performances, this great jazz & blues bar and restaurant offers live music shows every Friday at 4 p.m. and on weekends at 12 noon (a good time and place for afternoon drinks).

If you want to push it a block further east (off **Stroll 4** map), there's **Queen Mother Café** at 208. This cool restaurant serves tasty quality food in a relaxed (and loud) atmosphere.

8 On your way westbound along Queen Street, don't miss the area's landmark: the SUV popping out of the east wall of the **CTV** building (299).

9 In this section, I like to visit three unique shops: Latino **El Mundo** (230), avant-garde **John Fluevog Shoes** (242) and vintage **Tribal Rhythm** (248). **Café Crêpe** (246) offers good crêpes in a Parisian-like bistro decor.

10 Between John and Spadina, are my favourite stores in the area: zen **EKO** (288) offering a truly original jewelry selection, and whimsical **Fashion Crimes** (322) jammed floor to ceiling with ball gowns, cocktail dresses and accessories.

Spadina Avenue

11 Along Spadina Avenue, you will notice ear-shaped green signs on certain poles. They're part of a really cool urban project called *Murmur*. See **www.murmurtoronto.ca** for details.

These signs feature a number you can call on your cell to access a message from a local resident, giving you information about your surroundings.

12 Walk two minutes north on Spadina for a coffee break at **Dark Horse Espresso Bar** at 215 Spadina Avenue. See the vertical garden by the café's northern exit.

Grafitti Lane

13 South of Queen, turn west into the first lane you'll see off Spadina. From Spadina to Portland, a real outdoor gallery awaits. The first graffiti you see by Spadina are not the best. Keep going.

The mural you'll see on **Java House** at Augusta and Queen W fits right in. (They have a great patio.)

14 Continue in the alley past Augusta and you'll find a garden in the middle of this urban jungle.

Portland Street

At the end of the graffiti lane, you'll reach Portland.

15 I really like the breakfasts at funky **Sadie's Diner**, a 3-min walk south on Portland, at 504 Adelaide.

Check the beautiful home decor store/café **La Merceria** next door.

On the southwest corner of Portland and Queen, there's a huge **Joe Fresh** store in a beautiful **Loblaws** (with **Winners** on the second floor).

16 On the southeast corner, you'll find playful gift shop **Outer Layer** and two unique specialty stores: inspiring ribbon shop **Mokuba** (575 Queen E.) and studio/boutique **Wildhagen** selling designer hats for men and women upstairs.

Further west on Queen, past Ryerson, is **Shanghai Cowgirl** (538 Queen W.), with funky booths and a patio (great for lunch and a drink).

Wolseley Street

17 Alternative **Theatre Passe Muraille** has been around for ages but not many know where it actually is. Go north on Ryerson Ave. and you'll find the pretty heritage building located at the corner of Wolseley St. and Ryerson.

18 Keep walking east on Wolseley and you'll see fun murals on the back wall of the stores lined along the parking lot.

There's an amazing old building where Wolseley meets Denison Avenue.

Back to Queen

19 Walk south on Denison Avenue to get to Queen Street. Then walk east to get back to your starting point. One store should really catch your attention between Augusta and Spadina: eye-candy dress shop **Original** (515 Queen W.).

Revamped waterfront, renewed fun

There was a time when there wasn't much incentive to venture east of **Queen's Quay Terminal** to admire a few existing features: some public art, the point zero of Ontario's longest street (Yonge Street) marked with engraved brass letters on the sidewalk, and Redpath's whales mural. Then, new attractions started to appear in what is now called East Bayfront. First came **Sugar Beach** (with the pink umbrellas), followed by **Sherbourne Common** (with water sculptures and a canal redirecting treated water to the lake). Now, there's a tree-lined waterfront promenade with huge patio!

STROLL 5

Full loop:
3.9 km (1 hr)

Shorter version:
The section east of Lower Jarvis is only 1 km long (a 15-min walk) and it will allow you to enjoy the lovely waterfront promenade.

Game for more?
The **Queens Quay Harbourfront Stroll** (**Stroll 6**, p. 39) starts right where **Stroll 5** ends at **Queen's Quay Terminal**.

Parking & TTC
• From **Union Subway Station**, it will take you 15 minutes to walk to **Queen's Quay Terminal**.
• There are parking lots around **Sugar Beach**. At the time of print, **Against the Grain** said they'll deduct the parking fees from your bill if you park underground (in **Corus** building) on weekdays after 6 p.m. or on the weekends.
• **Loblaws**' customers who spend at least $10, can park for two hours.

Other TIPS
• **Sherbourne Common**'s spray pad turns into a rink in the winter.

Sherbourne Common

1 I prefer to park in the parking lot on the east part of **Stroll 5**. (The parking lot closer to **Sugar Beach** usually fills quickly.) From there, you'll only have to walk a few minutes along a boring stretch before reaching **Sherbourne Common**.

This park spreads north and south of the street. Its intriguing shiny building is not just an architectural statement, it's a facility for the treatment of storm water.

2 It filters and releases the water into an esthetic canal leading to the lake, thanks to three tall artistic structures located on the north side of Queens Quay.

The Promenade

3 Walk behind the building to access the waterfront promenade. It is paved with cobblestones baring a maple leaf pattern and lined with trees and designer benches (further west).

4 You'll pass in front of the new **George Brown College** campus and will reach the **Corus Entertainment** building featuring a great addition to the area: the **Against the Grain** restaurant with a huge waterfront patio. We've eaten there often and it was delicious.

Make sure you get a good look inside the **Corus** building for the school of iridescent Neon Tetra fish swimming from the ceiling, and the 4-storey-high flumeslide for the employees. Very Pixar-ish.

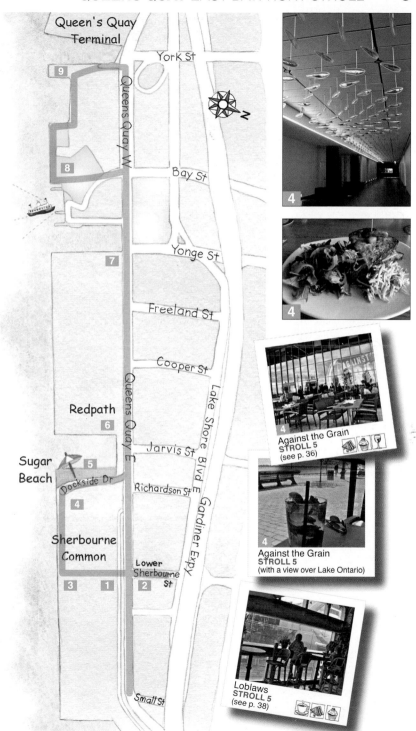

Against the Grain
STROLL 5
(see p. 36)

Against the Grain
STROLL 5
(with a view over Lake Ontario)

Loblaws
STROLL 5
(see p. 38)

5 **Canada's Sugar Beach** is the other welcome addition, with 36 permanent pink umbrellas, beach chairs, white sand and a cute spray pad. (The sprays are lit at night!)

Lower Jarvis Street

6 I've always liked to have a coffee by the windows on the second floor of the **Loblaws**. It's a vantage point to admire the beautiful turquoise mural of whales on the triangular facade of the **Redpath** sugar refinery, with shimmering Lake Ontario in the background.

Yonge Street

7 At the foot of Yonge, look down and you'll see brass letters inlaid in the sidewalk, confirming this is Canada's longest street.

Across the street is a huge metal sculpture to observe.

Ferry Ramp

8 The **Toronto Ferry**, allowing you to reach **Toronto Islands**, is just past the **Westin Harbour Castle**, at the foot of Bay Street.

For years, I passed by the park to the west of the ferry ramp without checking it out, assuming it was just a little uninteresting patch of greenery. What a mistake!

9 It actually offers a lovely stroll along the waterfront and leads to **Queen's Quay Terminal**, with an intriguing sphere. (You can explore in and around this structure.)

Harbourfront and beyond

There's so much going on at **Harbourfront Centre** that it's easy to moor there and forget about setting sail further west to admire what lies ahead: the sculptural **Simcoe WaveDeck** (which also serves as a stylish boardwalk), the yellow umbrellas of **HtO Park**, the **Toronto Music Garden**, the tall totem of **Little Norway Park** and the impressive installation in remote **Ireland Park** facing the **CN Tower** across the channel (a tribute to the 38,000 Irish immigrants who arrived here in 1847 to escape the Great Potato Famine). All of them by the water!

STROLL 6

Full loop:
4 km (1 hr)

Shorter version:
The unique (and less travelled) section of **Stroll 6** is found west of Lower Spadina Avenue (1.8 km long, a 30-min walk).

Game for more?
The **Lake Shore Land of the Giants Stroll** (**Stroll 3**, p. 23) includes Bathurst Street just a 5-min walk north of **Ireland Park** in **Stroll 6**.

Parking & TTC
• Streetcar **#511** going southbound on Bathurst stops near Lake Shore Blvd W.
• I usually go to the parking lot across from **Harbourfront**, off Lower Simcoe.
• There's a cheaper (but farther) indoor parking lot at the **Marina Quay West**, just west of **Toronto Music Garden**.

Other TIPS
• Go to **www.harbourfrontcentre.ca** to *What's On* section for a listing of the festivals, outdoor movies and shows (including the **Music Garden**'s).

York Street

1 I usually park across the street from **Harbourfront Centre** because the parking lots east of this one tend to be more expensive. From there, walk east, straight to the bustling southeast corner of York Street and Queens Quay. (Look down by the **Second Cup**, you'll see brass fish encased in the sidewalk.)

2 **Queen's Quay Terminal** is worth walking through, to admire the huge mezzanine with wall to wall glass windows.

I've really enjoyed a meal at the **Pearl Harbourfront** dim sum restaurant on the second floor. It's a place where they keep strolling by with the dumpling cart for you to choose from during peek lunch time. (There's no cart in the middle of the day but you'll have better chances to get a window table, truly blissful on a sunny day.)

3 The waterfront is lined with patios on one side, tour boats on the other. (I prefer **Bar Milano**'s patio for its two levels.)

Harbourfront Centre

Inside **Harbourfront Centre**, watch the artists in action in their studios on the east side of the building, and art displays on the west side.

4 Then walk to the south side to **Lakeside Eats**, with a lovely patio by the pond (and the seasonal **Splash Patio** by the lake). Both are licensed.

Walk around the big stage to reach the white bridge.

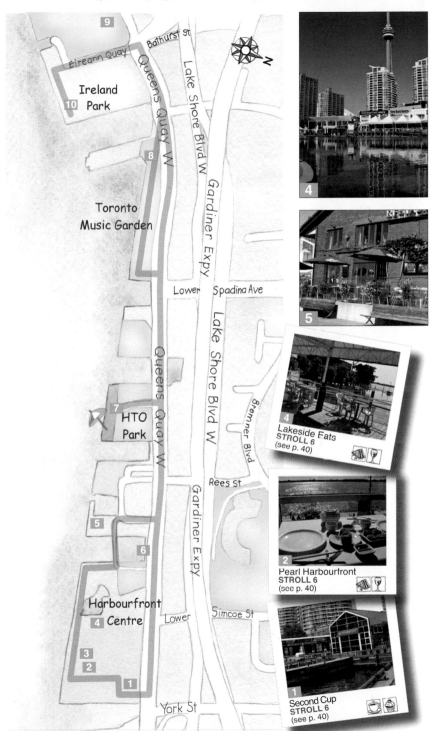

Eireann Quay

Bathurst St

Queens Quay W

Lake Shore Blvd W

9

Ireland
Park
10

8

Toronto
Music Garden

Gardiner Expy

Lower   Spadina Ave

Lake Shore Blvd W

Queens Quay W

7
HTO
Park

Bremner Blvd

Rees St

Gardiner Expy

5

6

Harbourfront
Centre
4

Lower   Simcoe St

3

2

1

York St

4

Lakeside Eats
STROLL 6
(see p. 40)

2

Pearl Harbourfront
STROLL 6
(see p. 40)

1

Second Cup
STROLL 6
(see p. 40)

41

5 At the time of print, **Amsterdam Brewery** was planning to occupy the large building with waterfront patio on the other side of the bridge.

6 The sculptured **Simcoe Wavedeck**, east of **PawsWay** (a place for pet lovers) by Queens Quay, is not to be missed.

HtO Park

7 You can't swim at this urban beach, further west, but it offers the fun combo of yellow umbrellas in the sand by the lake on one side, and the **CN Tower** on the other.

Music Garden

8 Simply gorgeous! You can rent a $7 audio wand for a 70-minute self-guided tour, at **Marina Quay West** near the garden's western entrance, to learn more about the musical theme.

Bathurst Street

9 **Little Norway Park**, across Bathurst, hosts a beautiful totem.

Walk down Bathurst and you'll reach **Toronto City Airport**. **Ireland Park** sits across from the airport.

10 The small patch of grass by the water is the entranceway to the quay, leading to a ship sculpture and life-size statues of emaciated Irish people overlooking downtown Toronto, a monument to over 38,000 Irish immigrants who reached Toronto by boat in 1847. (Construction is underway to create a park access from Queens Quay West.)

THE DISTILLERY
RED BRICK STROLL

Modern take on Victorian industry

It turns out it was a stroke of genius to save the Victorian industrial buildings left by the **Gooderham & Worts** empire and to refurbish them (leaving as much exposed brick as possible) into a slick historical haven with a cool mix of commercial and residential. The four-block site includes condos, art galleries, one-of-a-kind retail shops and restaurants. It is carless and peppered with huge pieces of art, with enough outdoor patios to admire it all, and plenty of nooks and crannies that will make you feel like you're exploring a European village.

STROLL 7

Full loop:
3.25 km (50 min)

Shorter version:
The Distillery itself is the main attraction of **Stroll 7**. From the parking lot, it will take you approximately 20 minutes to walk around the historic site (excluding all the stops, of course).

Game for more?
The **King East Design Stroll** (**Stroll 17**, p. 103) is parallel to **Stroll 7**, along King Street.

Parking & TTC
• The streetcar **#504** runs along King Street.
• There are parking lots at **The Distillery** (accessible off Parliament).
• There's a cheaper parking lot at the corner of The Esplanade and Berkeley Street (accessible from Front Street).

Other TIPS
• Go to the *Explore* section in www.thedistillerydistrict.com for a listing of the festivals and shows performed at the **Young Centre for the Performing Arts**.

The Distillery
This national historic site includes over forty red brick buildings proclaimed "the best preserved collection of Victorian industrial architecture in North America".

1   It is fun to enter it from Gristmill Lane (off Parliament, just south of Mill Street), where you'll see a modern glass version of a "flatiron building" near the weirdest faceless aluminium creature.

There are plenty of inspiring galleries along this lane such as **Engine Gallery** and **Pikto**.

2   A bit further, you'll meet another piece of modern art: a giant spider-like structure.

3   You'll have to explore the beautiful **Thomson Landry Gallery** with a French industrial feeling, across from **A Taste of Quebec**, a cheese place attached to another gallery owned by **Thomson Landry Gallery**.

4   My girlfriends agree that the best way to start this stroll is to do a beeline through this lane to grab a coffee at **Balzac's Coffee** (hidden behind yet another strange large-scale art installation).

We love it for its amazing chandelier and the tables in the mezzanine.

5   Near **Balzac** is Case Goods Lane where you'll find **Caffe Furbo**, much more minimalist

Walk down this lane to access **Artscape Case Goods Warehouse** with all the artist studios.

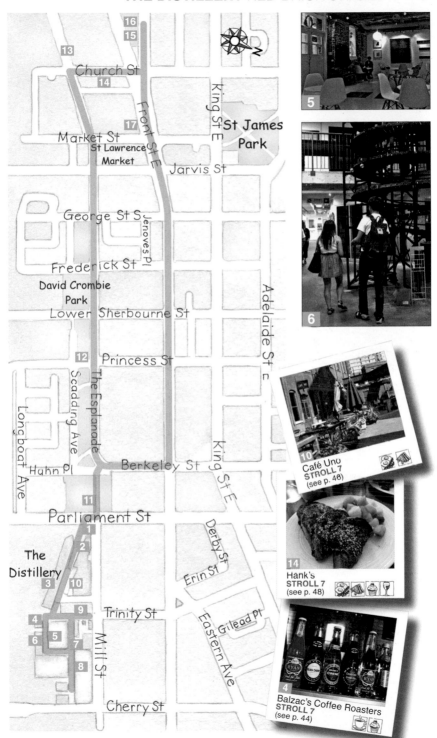

Church St

King St E

St James Park

Front St E

Market St

St Lawrence Market

Jarvis St

George St S

Jenoves Pl

Frederick St

David Crombie Park

Lower Sherbourne St

Adelaide St n

Princess St

The Esplanade

Scadding Ave

Longboat Ave

Berkeley St

King St E

Hahn Pl

Parliament St

The Distillery

Derby St

Erin St

Trinity St

Gilead Pl

Mill St

Eastern Ave

Cherry St

Café Uno
STROLL 7
(see p. 46)

Hank's
STROLL 7
(see p. 48)

Balzac's Coffee Roasters
STROLL 7
(see p. 44)

7 At the end of the lane, you'll turn into a cute alley with funky chairs and patios with flowers during the summer. It will lead you to Tank House Lane.

Turn right for more shops to explore, including my favourite place for last minute gifts for those who have everything: **Bergo Designs**.

8 Further, just before the **Young Centre for the Performing Arts**, is **SOMA Chocolate & Gelato**, one of the few artisanal shops in Toronto making its own chocolate from cocoa beans. Among my favourite treats: their thick and spicy hot chocolate (so soothing during a visit in the fall) and any of their chocolate-covered fruit.

Walking back towards the main lane, Trinity Street, you'll find **Brick Street Bakery** to your right, with a cute outdoor patio (their sausage rolls are decadent). Across the lane is **Lileo**, offering the best of everything: clothes, books, footwear and lifestyle accessories, in a brilliant display. Everything is expensive in that store but it is the perfect place to browse with girlfriends.

9 Also along Trinity Street are **Gotstyle Menswear** and **Corktown Designs**, filled with interesting jewelry, and eclectic **Blackbird Vintage Finds**. (Didn't know where at the time of print but expect **Fleuvog Shoes**!)

10 I've tried many patios all around **The Distillery**. Each of them has its own "personality". Price wise, there's **Café Uno**

on your way back through Distillery Lane, which does a good job with its affordable and tasty sandwiches (and many more food options).

The Esplanade

11 The reason I chose to call this the "red brick" stroll is that the sidewalk linking **The Distillery** to the **St. Lawrence Market** is lined with reddish brick, starting at **Parliament Square,** just across Parliament Street.

At the end of this path, you'll see the **Canadian Stage Company**'s lovely red brick building (also hosting the **Théâtre français de Toronto**).

12 Through the 10-min walk along The Esplanade, you'll see fountains, playgrounds, a wading pool and a garden in the **David Crombie Park**.

Lower Jarvis Street

Where the red brick-lined sidewalk stops, the **St. Lawrence Market** (with over 100 merchants) takes over. The south market in this red building is closed on Sundays and Mondays and the north market located just across Front Street is open on the weekends.

Church Street

13 Keep strolling west on The Esplanade to Church Street. Beyond this street, The Esplanade is lined with patios on one side and **Novotel**'s chic Parisian arches on the other.

14 At 9 Church Street awaits a trio of restaurants belonging to the same owners. With friends,

I've enjoyed a tasty breakfast at **Hank's**. We've gorged on fries from **GBK**, and have indulged a few times in a fancy meal at the counter of the **Wine Bar** (about to revamp its decor).

Front Street

15 At the corner of Front and Church is Toronto's historic landmark the **Flatiron Building**. (New York also has one but it was built after Toronto's.)

There's a direct link between **The Distillery** and **Flatiron**. Its official name is the **Gooderham Building**, as in Gooderham & Worts distillery. It was built in 1892 and served as the distillers' offices for 60 years.

Make sure you check the back of the **Flatiron Building**. It features a very cool trompe-l'oeil reproducing the building across Front Street, currently home to a **Winners**.

16 There's a European feeling to this block facing **Berczy Park**.

17 The stretch along Front Street going eastbound from this park to the **St. Lawrence Market** at Lower Jarvis Street is lovely.

Market Square, the small plaza just west of the building adorned with a large mural, includes the **Rainbow Cinema Market Square** (with $5 Tuesdays and $7.50 matinees).

Keep walking east for a peek at one more red brick item: the imposing **Canadian Opera Company** building, before turning right on Berkeley to return to your starting point.

UNIVERSITY OF TORONTO
IVY LEAGUE STROLL

The inner beauty of U of T

Once you've walked through the stone arches and into the hidden courtyards of the majestic **University of Toronto**, you'll discover that there's a bit of Harry Potter's Hogwarts in it. Without a doubt, U of T should qualify as an Ivy League university. Beautiful ivy is rampant on the old walls of the buildings throughout the campus! (And it all looks even better during the fall). The **Philosopher's Walk** will lead you to Bloor Street where more major league architecture is awaiting right and left: the **Royal Ontario Museum** and the **Royal Conservatory**.

STROLL
8

Full loop:
5.2 km (1 hr 20 min)

Shorter version:
For a shorter stroll of 3.4 km (50 min), stick to the circuit west of **Queen's Park** and go directly to Tower Road instead of taking Hoskin and St. George.

Game for more?
The **Yorkville V.I.P. Stroll** (**Stroll 28**, p. 167) is just 2 minutes east of this stroll, north of Bloor West.

Parking & TTC
• Exit at **Museum** or **Queen's Park Subway Stations**.
• There's a large **Green P** parking lot on Bedford St., north of Bloor, across from the **Conservatory**.

Other TIPS
• General admission to the **ROM** is $9 instead of $15 for adults on Fridays after 4:30 p.m. (closing at 8:30 p.m.). It is $6 instead of $12 for kids.
• For the listing of shows at the **Royal Conservatory**, go to *Performance* on **www.rcmusic.ca**.

Bloor Street West

1 After parking in the municipal parking lot on Bedford Street, cross to the south side of Bloor. You could enter the **Royal Conservatory** to your left (273 Bloor West) to have a delicious breakfast or lunch at **b Espresso Bar**. It is located in the stunning atrium of the conservatory and opens at 8 a.m. Monday to Friday, 9 a.m. Saturdays, 11 a.m. on Sundays.

Or you could walk west on Bloor to have a fancier bite at **L'Espresso Bar Mercurio** (321 Bloor West). It feels luxurious, with all the long drapes and columns and features a lovely garden patio. I was told that many **U of T** professors eat here. (They open at 7:30 a.m. Monday to Friday and at 9 a.m. on the weekends.)

Then you're good to go for this exciting stroll.

2 Walk right on Bloor and turn right again on the **Philosopher's Walk**, through the black iron gates by the crystal shape of the **ROM**.

Trinity College

3 You should access **Trinity College** from this path but for a more dramatic effect, I suggest you turn right on Hoskin Avenue and enter the imposing building from its main entrance.

Make sure you don't miss the carved details all around, such as the funny professors' heads on each side of the doorways. (Doesn't one of them look like John Lennon?)

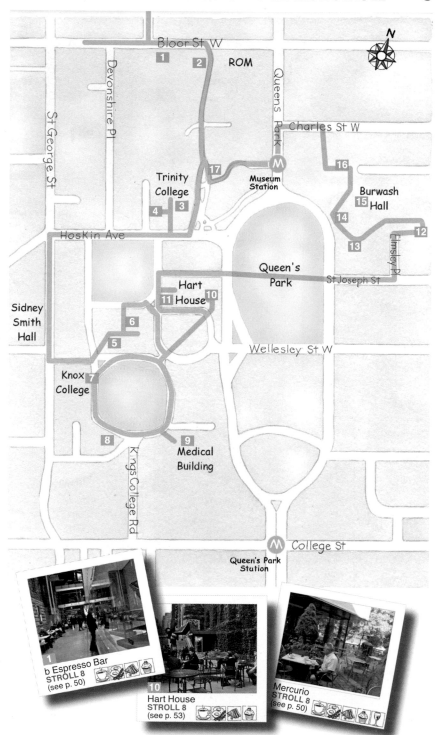

N

Bloor St W

1

2

ROM

Devonshire Pl

St George St

Queens Park

Charles St W

17

Museum Station

M

16

Burwash Hall

15

14

13

12

Elmsley Pl

Trinity College

4   3

Hoskin Ave

Queen's Park

St Joseph St

Sidney Smith Hall

Hart House

11   10

6

5

Wellesley St W

Knox College

7

8

9

Medical Building

Kings College Rd

M

Queen's Park Station

College St

1
b Espresso Bar
STROLL 8
(see p. 50)

10
Hart House
STROLL 8
(see p. 53)

Mercurio
STROLL 8
(see p. 50)

Walk through the building to enter the magnificent courtyard with a unique patterned path (which is even more spectacular in the fall when the grass is shorter). This type of open air space surrounded by buildings on all sides is called a quadrangle.

4 On your way back to the front door, take the corridor on your right to discover another hidden treasure: the elegant chapel of **Trinity College**. This gem of unpretentious beauty is the last design of the English architect who created the Liverpool Cathedral and... the British red phone booths!

Kings College Circle

Walk right on Hoskin Avenue, then left on St. George Street, into the campus. Facing Willcocks Street, past **Sidney Smith Hall**, you'll see a lane on your left. It leads to Kings College Circle.

5 Take that lane and walk left, around the little round building. Then pass through the arch of the majestic building and you'll come to another fantastic quadrangle.

6 Keep walking through the series of wooden arches to your left.

Turn right to Tower Road, then right again, to return to Kings College Circle, which you should start touring on your right.

This section of the stroll is truly spectacular during the fall, when the ivy covering the heritage buildings all around the circle changes colour.

7 **Knox College**'s facade is breathtaking. And you must enter it to admire the courtyard through the cloister's gothic windows (an apt architectural choice considering this College grants theology degrees).

8 The domed rotunda of the grand **Convocation Hall** is not bad either!

9 It is fun to contrast all this classical architecture with the modern take of the **Medical Sciences Building** at 1 Kings College Circle. (Walk around the building to the left of the entrance for some interesting modern art.)

10 Back to your starting point on the circle, walk through the park on your right to get to **Hart House**. (From that park, you can see the mural under the viaduct to your right, at the intersection of Queen's Park and Wellesley.)

Walk up the stairs to the east of the building to discover a deer cutout on the stone balcony.

Hart House includes a cafeteria with a wide range of affordable food options and an outdoor patio.

11 Turn right on Tower Road (peeking into the classy courtyard of **Hart House** on your way). Past the face sculpture offering an amusing optical illusion, turn right into the lane to reach **Queen's Park**.

Elmsley Place

Carefully cross the street and walk through **Queen's Park** to get to St. Joseph Street and turn left on Elmsley Place.

12 Here, it feels more like a village than a campus. Especially if you turn right past the houses to reach the church.

13 At the church, turn left into the narrow path with a flower garden. It leads to a large courtyard. Walk through the arch behind the geometrical metal sculpture, then right again, around the **Pontifical Institute**.

Burwash Hall

14 My favourite spot on the campus east of Queen's Park Crescent is the pond by **Burwash Hall**. You'll need to cross the path by the statue of the two ladies and pass betwen two buildings to reach the series of Neo-Gothic student housing covered in ivy.

15 Weather permitting, you'll be greeted by the cheerful sound of water falling into the pond.

16 A bit further, to your left, you can't miss the majestic building of **Victoria University**. Around it, to your left, you'll notice the statue of a crucified woman by **Emmanuel College**.

17 Keep walking towards Charles Street, then turn left and take the underpass to reach the **Royal Ontario Museum** on the west side of the street. Walk south, past the white dome and its adjacent building, and cut through the passageway to the right of the **Faculty of Law** (the building with four large columns). It will take you back to the **Philosopher's Walk**.

It was there all along!

Most people visiting the **Eaton Centre** are unaware of the hidden treasures surrounding it. When you walk around **Yonge-Dundas**, it feels like our own little Times Square. There's indeed a buzz to the place, with the line-up of activities at the square, the numerous animated billboards and the huge crowd gathering at the 4-way crosswalk of Yonge and Dundas. But walk a bit further northeast into the campus of **Ryerson University**, or just west of the shopping mall, and you'll find water fountains, labyrinth, church and beauty in quiet public places.

STROLL 9

Full loop:
2.5 km (40 min)

Shorter version:
For a 1.5 km stroll (25 min) covering the best hidden treasures, walk north of the parking lot on Victoria, then east on Gould and enter the **Kerr Hall West**'s courtyard. Then walk back to **Yonge-Dundas Square**, enter the **Eaton Centre** and exit through the west door by Sears to **Trinity Square**.

Game for more?
The **City Hall Green Roof Stroll** (**Stroll 11**, p. 67) is just across from **Trinity Square**.

Parking & TTC
• Exit at **Queen** or **Dundas Subway Stations**.
• The parking lot on Victoria Street, just north of Dundas is less expensive than the **Eaton Centre**'s.

Other TIPS
• For a list of events at **Yonge-Dundas Square**, see **www.ydsquare.ca**.
• Go to **www.music-mondays.ca** for the free shows in **Trinity Square**'s church.

Victoria Street

1 When you're visiting, don't miss the dead-end at the foot of Victoria, with inviting tables and chairs. You're entering **Ryerson University**'s hub.

Devonian Square is an amazing urban sight, with its large boulders and reflecting pool turning into a rink in the winter.

The adjacent **Ryerson Image Centre** illuminates at night, and the colours are ever changing! Pure free urban fun.

2 Turn right on Gould Street and enter **Kerr Hall West**'s courtyard on your left. You'll soon see something unique: the facade of a whole historic building standing in the park, with the sky showing through its windows.

3 Go through the courtyard to access Gerrard Street on the other side. Walk left around the building and follow the green path of **Ryerson Community Park** leading back to Gould Street. It includes a fountain and some art on the buildings. (On the way, on Edward Street, the first street to your right, is the **World's Biggest Book Store**.)

Yonge-Dundas Square
Turn east to Yonge Street, then south.

4 There's a buzz to Yonge-Dundas, with the line-up of activities at the square, the numerous animated billboards and the crowd gathering at the crosswalk, one of a few in Toronto where pedestrians can cross diagonally).

5 When there's room left by the other activities going on (multicultural markets, shows, etc), you can see twenty water fountains spurting from the ground.

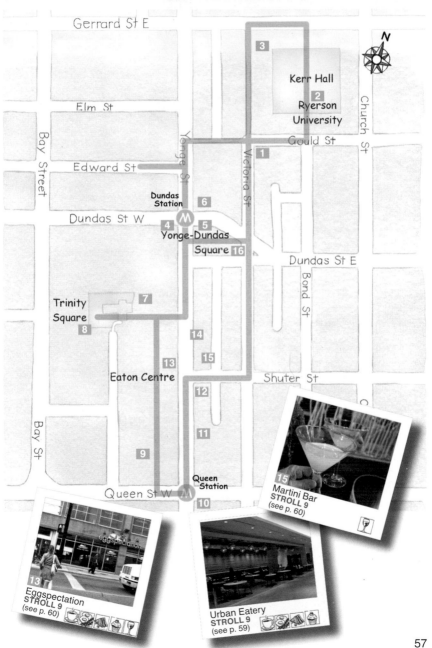

Eggspectation
STROLL 9
(see p. 60)

Urban Eatery
STROLL 9
(see p. 59)

Martini Bar
STROLL 9
(see p. 60)

6 North of the square is the **Yonge & Dundas** movie theatre complex (formerly **AMC**), including a food court with a view and a few restaurants. I've had a chance to enjoy the outdoor patio of the **Milestones** restaurant on the third floor and it offered a great view over the square.

Trinity Square

Going from the chaotic techno fun of **Yonge-Dundas Square** to the historical oasis of **Trinity Square** is like experiencing time travel. To fully enjoy the contrast, enter into the **Eaton Centre** from the Yonge entrance by **Roots** (past Sears) and go straight ahead. Then exit the mall from the other side (**Sears** will be on your right) to enter another world!

7 Just turn right and you'll discover a paved courtyard with an old fountain surrounded by stone buildings which are muffling the noise from the street. It feels like we're in the public space of a small European village.

The unassuming **Trinity Square Café**, located in the back of the church, is managed by a non-profit community mental health agency. It is only open on weekdays from 11:30 a.m. to 2:30 p.m. but it offers tasty and affordable homemade food.

8 Enter into the **Church of the Holy Trinity** to admire its painted ceiling. (Note that free summer concerts are usually offered at 12:15 p.m. on Mondays.)

Trinity Square features one of the loveliest fountains in Toronto, with water overflowing into a small canal simulating a stream. (South of the pool is a unique labyrinth made of contrasting bricks.)

Eaton Centre

9 Go to the lower level to have a look at **Urban Eatery**, **Eaton Centre**'s new and very classy food court. Then, back to the main floor, walk south and past the fountain to see the sixty geese art installation *Flightstop*, by artist Michael Snow. (I recommend admiring them from the glass elevator.)

10 Exit to Queen Street for another impressive piece of art inside the building at the southeast corner of Queen and Yonge. Suspended over the escalator, the sculpture itself looks like a distorted stairway to heaven.

Yonge Street

Walking north on Yonge, you'll pass the ornate facade of the old-fashioned **Elgin and Winter Garden Theatre**.

11 It is evident that the next two majestic buildings have seen better days and are searching for a new raison d'être but they are still beautiful.

12 There's a café at the corner of Yonge and Shuter: **ING Direct Downtown Toronto Café** (ING hadn't yet changed its name at the time of print). Yes, from the street, it looks like a bank but there's more to it. Inside, if you

pass the flat screens promoting the bank's products, you'll see a very slick design, a vertical green garden, comfy sofas and an environmentally friendly counter. Upstairs, they manage the **Network Orange**, a fantastic new concept of office space sharing. Ask to check it out to see how gorgeous it is.

13 Across the street is **Eggspectation**, a vast all-day breakfast place (220 Yonge).

14 If you feel ready for lunch, I suggest the mezzanine of **Paramount**, a popular middle eastern restaurant at 253 Yonge. The ground level is busy but the lovely mezzanine is a cosier space, where many hijab-clad girlfriends retreat (note that it closes after lunch until dinner).

Back to Victoria

15 I recently had the opportunity to have an afternoon drink at the **Martini Bar** in the **Pantages Hotel Toronto Centre** at 200 Victoria Street and really loved the dark modern lounge of this luxury boutique hotel. They offer over 40 martini recipes at varying prices but every day from 3 p.m. to 6 p.m., there are six options at $6.

This is a favourite pre-theatre stop for those attending the productions of nearby **Elgin Theatre** on Yonge, **Massey Hall** on Shuter or **Ed Mirvish Theatre** on Victoria.

16 Keep walking north to reach your starting point near **Yonge-Dundas Square** and all its vibrant activities.

Long walk, for long conversations

You can walk and talk and get deep into conversation with your girlfriends without fear of getting lost along this straight-line stroll. **Kay Gardner Beltline Park** is Toronto's longest and narrowest park (so narrow in fact, that you won't see it on a regular map). Trees lining it on both sides form arches over our heads on many parts of the trail, making it the best fall outing for girlfriends. Running through posh neighbourhoods, it once was a train track built by private interest to solve commuter transportation problems in the 1890's. When you're ready to get back to civilization, there's a lovely stretch of Eglinton West to explore.

STROLL
10

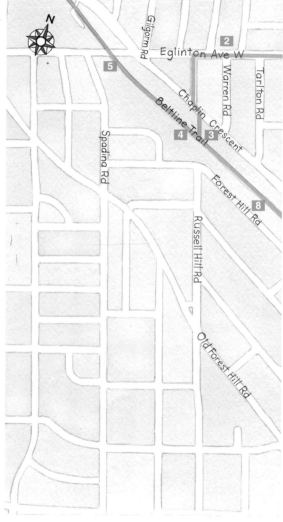

Full loop:
9.6 km (2 h 30 min)

Shorter version:
Walk just a bit past the bridge (west of the trail entrance near Russel Hill Rd.) or up to Avenue Rd. (east of the entrance by Duncannon) for a nice 2.5 km stroll (40 min).

Game for more?
Take the entrance to the **Mount Pleasant Cemetery** along the trail (on the east side of Yonge). Keep your left to reach the central garden (part of the **Rosedale Meandering Stroll** (**Stroll 24**, p. 143).

Parking & TTC
• Exit at **Davisville Subway Station**.
• Easy to find free parking on weekends. On weekdays (9 a.m. to 4 p.m.) try Chaplin Crescent, west of Duncannon Dr. or go to the **Green P** on Castle Knock Rd., north of Eglinton.

Other TIPS
• You can access the trail from Mount Pleasant, Yonge, Oriole Park, Avenue Road and Bathurst.

Eglinton Avenue
1 It's usually easy to find free parking on weekdays along the streets north and south of Eglinton Avenue West. On weekends, I prefer to cut to the chase and go straight to the municipal parking lot at Castle Knock Road, north of Eglinton (not far from **Phipps Bakery** and **Tea Emporium**).

13
Tea Emporium
STROLL 10
(see p. 66)

14
Phipps Bakery
STROLL 10
(see p. 66)

2
Hotel Gelato
STROLL 10
(see p. 64)

Burnaby Blvd

Castle Knock Rd

1 14 12

Eglinton Ave W

13

Duncannon Dr

Elmsthorpe Ave

Braemar Ave

Highbourne Rd

Avenue Rd

Oriole Pkwy

Eastbourne Ave

Beltline Trail

Larratt St

Forest Hill Road Park

Chaplin Crescent

Imperia

Dunvegan Rd

Forest Hill Rd

Avenue Rd

Oxton Ave

Davisville Station Ⓜ

Oriole Park

Yonge St

Killbarry Rd

Lasce

1

2

2

2 If you just want to grab a coffee to go before your stroll, there's hip **Mad Bean** (519 Eglinton West). But if you want to take your time, try **Hotel Gelato** (532 Eglinton West). This glam café is licensed and serves great breakfasts (treats, lunch and dinner). Everything is served with a charming attention to details.

3 Then, walk down Russel Hill Road, and left on Chaplin Crescent to reach the entrance to the **Kay Gardner Beltline Trail** on your right and let the fun begin!

West Beltline Trail

4 The **Beltline Trail** is heaven for joggers, bikers and walkers.

The path is wide and lined with greenery all along. It is part of what used to be a private railway line completed in 1892 (which closed its passenger service only two years later due to the depression in the 1890's).

The City of Toronto bought part of the abandoned railway in 1972 to make a park, thanks to the work of City Councillor Kay Gardner, hence the name.

5 Turn right (westbound) on the **Beltline Trail** and you'll soon come across the staircase leading up to Eglinton Avenue West (a good little workout going up and down if you want to check the view from above).

6 Past this point and up to Bathurst Street is not the best part of the trail. But right after, you'll once again feel sheltered by the trees, which create a pleasing natural tunnel.

7 You'll pass the small **Nicol MacNicol Parkette** before reaching the western end of the **Beltline Trail**, at Allen Road.

You can now do the 2-km walk back to the trail's entrance by Russel Hill Road and finish your stroll, or keep going further east on the trail.

East Beltline Trail

8 East of the trail's entrance by Russel Hill Road, it's a 4.8-km return loop to the eastern end of the **Kay Gardner Beltline Trail**. The trees are more imposing in this section of the trail and you get a glimpse of the backyards of impressive properties.

9 After a little while, past Avenue Road, you'll reach the pedestrian bridge running over Yonge Street. (On the east side of Yonge is a staircase to get down to the street level.)

10 Along the trail, you will find two entrances to **Mount Pleasant Cemetery**.

11 Elegant condos now line the path on your left. The trail ends at Mount Pleasant, which you can reach from a staircase. From there, it is a 2-km walk back to a path linking the trail to Chaplin Crescent, just east of Duncannon Drive.

Back to Eglinton

Walk north on Duncannon to get back to Eglinton Avenue West.

12 If you still have the energy, the .6-km stretch between Duncannon Drive and Highbourne Road is full of great shops selling clothing, fashion or home accessories.

13 Two blocks east on Eglinton awaits the only **Tea Emporium** that I know with a lounge (351 Eglinton West). And a very lovely one at that, which feels and smells like a spa lounge. Their exotic ice teas are perfect in the summer. A small hourglass accompanies their hot teas to ensure it is steeped just right.

14 Check **Phipps Bakery Café** (420 Eglinton West) as you walk back to Castle Knock Road. Their mural in the back of the shop is truly cheerful. (Their mac & cheese or soup of the day are perfect after a stroll during the fall.)

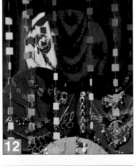

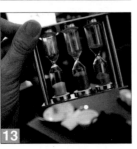

This stroll is over the top!

This is actually a 2-for-1 rooftop stroll if you start your mini-adventure at the **Sheraton Hotel**, across the street from **City Hall**. From its lobby, you'll be able to access the outdoor **Waterfall Gardens** on higher floors, for a first taste of a green roof, with a small waterfall as a bonus. Then, you'll find a passage linking the hotel to the U-shaped raised platform of **City Hall**. It will take you to the half-kilometre path which circumnavigates **City Hall Podium Green Roof**.

STROLL 11

Full loop:
2.5 km (40 min)

Shorter version:
For a 1.3 km version (20 min), simply walk from the **City Hall** indoor parking lot, up the ramp, around the green roof, and back.

Game for more?
The **Yonge Street Hidden Treasures Stroll** (**Stroll 9**, p. 55) includes **Trinity Square**, just across from **City Hall**, on the east side of Bay Street.

Parking & TTC
• Exit at **Osgoode Subway Station**.
• There's a parking lot (no cheap option in the area) under **City Hall**, with an entrance off Queen, on the west end of the square.

Other TIPS
• The **Canadian Opera Company** offers free concerts at the **Four Seasons Centre** (visit *Performances & Tickets* on **www.coc.ca**). The first-come first-served shows are at 12 noon on many weekdays from September to June (box office opens at 11:30 a.m.).

Osgoode Hall

1 Before starting your green roof stroll at the **Sheraton Hotel**, I thought I'd introduce you to a gem people pass by everyday. Once you've parked in the parking lot under **City Hall**, walk right on Queen Street to enter the grounds of **Osgoode Hall** through the elegant black iron gates.

2 The general public is allowed to visit this heritage building, surrounded by a beautiful garden. It gets even better inside, with original tiling on a spectacular floor and exquisite work on the ceiling amidst the arches.

3 Back on Queen, look up to the northwest at University Avenue to see **Canada Life**'s weather beacon. Its lights are running up when the temperature is getting warmer.

4 On the south side of Queen, you can admire the elegance of the **Four Seasons Centre**, home to the **COC** and the **National Ballet**. (Read the **TIPS** section about weekday free concerts presented in the **Richard Bradshaw Amphitheatre** on the 2nd floor.)

5 Further south on University is your chance to see the amazing dragon-like sculpture *Rising*, attached to the new luxury hotel **Shangri-La**.

Then walk east on Queen to reach the **Sheraton Centre Toronto Hotel** (123 Queen West), which included a green roof way before **City Hall**. (You can see its trees from **City Hall**'s ramp.)

Sheraton Hotel

Link@Sheraton Café is a little convenience store with counter food inside the **Sheraton Hotel**, which sells **Starbucks** coffee (at $3 a regular cup!) and has a few tables facing the 30-foot-high bay windows, with a view into the courtyard.

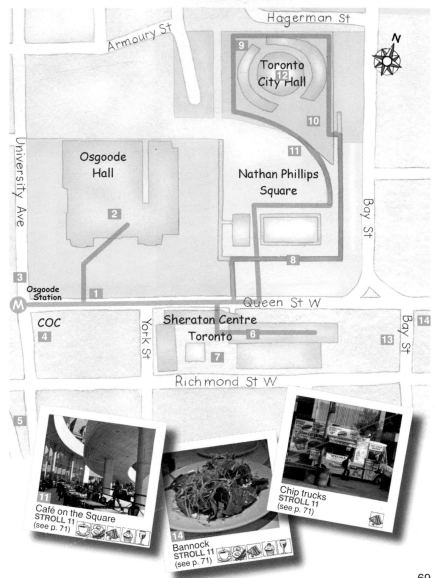

Café on the Square
STROLL 11
(see p. 71)

Bannock
STROLL 11
(see p. 71)

Chip trucks
STROLL 11
(see p. 71)

6 Use the escalators to reach the impressive outdoor **Waterfall Garden**, two floors higher (yes, it features a waterfall).

You can walk all around the outdoor mezzanine to explore nooks and crannies around the reflecting pools.

7 Stairs by the entrance lead to a higher green roof with trees and garden. (The guests' indoor and outdoor pools are located on the southwest corner of this floor.)

Return to the lower floor inside the hotel, and follow the signs for the Queen Tower to your right. That's where you'll find the door leading to the pedestrian bridge. (Note that it's usually locked from the outside. Once you're out, you're out.)

8 The **Sheraton**'s pedestrian bridge links the hotel to **City Hall**'s mezzanine ramp.

The branch of the ramp to your left will eventually give access to a new two-storey restaurant being built in **Nathan Phillips Square**. Take the branch to your right, walk around the square and reach the stairs at the end of the ramp to climb up to the green roof. The podium is the part of **City Hall** which looks like a spaceship.

Podium Green Roof

9 I visited it in spring, summer and fall. There were not many flowers but the gardens looked amazing and elegant, with an emphasis on texture as opposed to colour.

A concrete path runs around the green roof in a .5 km loop. We noticed that squirrels had adopted the place in the northeast corner of the roof, closer to the trees. (I could see the top of the **Church of the Holy Trinity** when looking further east from that corner.)

10 Many benches with built-in roofs have been installed for the benefit of those who want to eat their lunch in this oasis.

11 You could get a take-out (on weekdays) from the cafeteria-like **Café on the Square** on the ground level of **City Hall** or grab good old greasy fries and hotdogs from the chip trucks waiting for customers along Queen West.

While you're there

12 After a tour around **Nathan Phillips Square**, have a look inside **City Hall** to admire the mural of nails to your right by the entrance, the large model of the city to your left and the podium in the middle.

13 I suggest you end your stroll with a stop at classy **Ben McNally Books**, an amazing independent bookstore often missed because it's one block south of Queen, at 366 Bay Street.

14 We had a fancy lunch in the slick dinning room of **Bannock**, at the corner of Bay and Queen. Everything was delectable (best chic poutine ever!). They also serve lighter fare in their stylish grab-and-go café section with patio.

DON VALLEY
EVERGREEN BRICK WORKS STROLL
12

Real oasis in the middle of the city

You can do this stroll the easy way. Just park your car in one of the large parking lots (constructed to accommodate the increased flow of visitors to the new green urban development), go straight to the **Farmers' Market** or the **Café Belong** to gorge on yummy food, then casually walk on the boardwalk overlooking the marsh... Or you can make it more challenging, arriving on foot from the ravine path connecting to **Evergreen Brick Works** on either side of the site. (This way, you'll really deserve those scrumptious treats from the **Café** or the **Market**!)

STROLL
12

Full loop:
3.7 km (55 min)

Shorter version:
If you park at **Evergreen Brick Works**, the stroll will drop to 2 km (a 30-min walk).

Game for more?
If you keep walking north on the **Moore Ravine** trail (instead of walking up the trail to **Chorley Park**) you'll see the pedestrian bridge included in the **Rosedale Meandering Stroll** (**Stroll 24**, p. 143).

Parking & TTC
• Catch a free shuttle bus to **Evergreen** from the parkette just north of **Broadview Subway Station** (for schedule, go to **www.ebw.evergreen.ca** under *Visit*).
• Count around $6 to park in the lots of the **Brick Works**.
• Read #1 on parking near **Chorley Park**.

Other TIPS
• Their dynamic **Farmers' Market** is open year-round on Saturdays from 9 a.m. to 1 p.m. (open at 8 a.m. from May to end of October).

Chorley Park

1 My favourite way to access the **Don Valley Evergreen Brick Works** is from **Chorley Park**. First of all, it is only a 10-min. walk from the attraction. Then, there's plenty of free street parking along Douglas Drive and on nearby streets north of Douglas. And finally, since it lies on the top of the valley, it offers a great view over the complex.

2 Note that the dirt path leading down towards **Brick Works** is steep and might not be for everyone. It takes you to the **Moore Park Ravine** trail.

3 Turn right on this trail and you'll soon see **Evergreen Brick Works** through a clearing.

Brick Works

4 A couple of years ago, we needed to see the bricks mingle with the sand and pebbles on the paths to remind us there was a brick factory for a whole century on this site. Not anymore.

Thanks to the massive development project managed by **Evergreen**, all deteriorating heritage buildings have been salvaged and integrated into an exciting showcase of urban green design.

When you reach the site, walk directly to the central building (called the Pavilions) and walk through it, to admire the art works greeting visitors. The iron panels with animal cutouts enclosed between brick walls are truly beautiful.

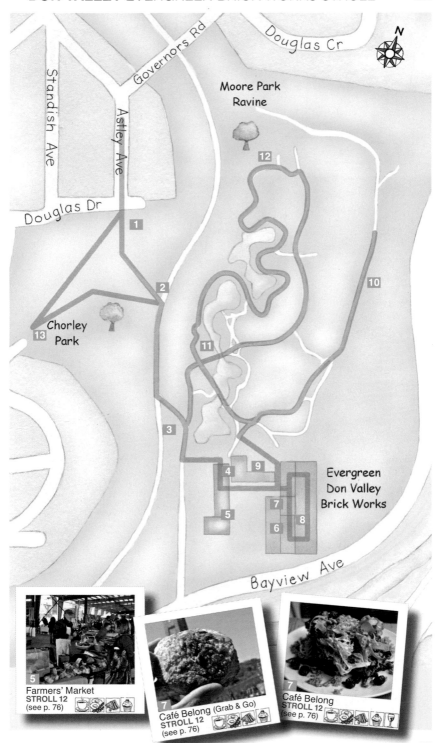

Governors Rd

Douglas Cr

Standish Ave

Astley Ave

Douglas Dr

N

Moore Park
Ravine

12

1

2

10

Chorley
Park

13

11

3

4 **9**

5

7

8

6

Evergreen
Don Valley
Brick Works

Bayview Ave

Farmers' Market
STROLL 12
(see p. 76)

Café Belong (Grab & Go)
STROLL 12
(see p. 76)

Café Belong
STROLL 12
(see p. 76)

Beyond those panels is a sculpture hanging from the ceiling, which made me feel like we were under the cracked ice of a river.

5 This is where you'll find the **Farmers' Market**. It runs year-round on Saturdays until 1 p.m.

Amidst the usual organic fruit and vegetables and craft offerings, expect delicious breakfasts and lunches to go, great coffee from the **Merchants of Green Coffee** (they have a stand there), and plenty of other treats.

6 If you missed the **Farmers' Market**, don't worry, you can always go to the permanent Marketplace under the roof, selling a wide range of merchandise including preserves, cook books, crafts and plants.

7 The industrial decor of **Café Belong** blends perfectly with the sculpture of Toronto's watershed we can admire from the bay windows. It opens at 11:30 a.m. for lunch, and 11 a.m. for weekend brunch (they have a patio).

All the items on their fancy menu are top quality and most are expensive but you can stop at their **Grab & Go** counter (open at last 9 a.m. to 5 p.m.) for their great coffee and affordable treats and light meals which you can eat near the Marketplace.

8 In and around the main building, you'll find the old factory's brick kilns, pass a plaza (which turns into a rink in the winter) and you'll notice plenty of funky hints to the industrial origin of the place.

9 By the tall chimney, they've developed an interactive section for kids.

10 Beyond, you'll notice a trail running up the hill to a sort of belvedere offering a grand panorama of the site. We've followed that trail. It runs all around the old quarry and provides another great view of the meandering path around the pond.

The trail then fades into the woods, with an unofficial link reaching the **Moore Ravine** trail below.

Note that this extra segment adds 1 km to the stroll.

Brick Works Trails

11 The **Don Valley Brick Works** still feels like a precious enclave hidden in the big mega city as soon as you walk past the chimney.

Strolling along the boardwalk and through the paths is a real pleasure. We can often see cranes by the water. Whole sections of the pond are filled with water lilies.

12 In the back of the park, we could mistake the walls of the old quarry for a natural escarpment shielding us from the urban noise.

Moore Ravine Park

13 Back on the **Moore Ravine** trail, turn right to return to **Chorley Park**. When you reach the path leading up to the park, you can choose to take the other path you'll see left of it. It will lead you to a long staircase which will take you to the west part of **Chorley Park**.

A real cliffhanger

This is the stroll with The View. Grab yourself coffee and treats in the last part of **The Beach** and head to **Rosetta Gardens**, a 10-minute drive away. As you stand on the edge of the gardens, imagine you're overlooking the ocean (an easy thing to do with the endless horizon and the turquoise shades of the water under the sun). Then, follow the trail east of **Rosetta** and down to the beach, for a totally different view of the white cliffs. This stroll will also take you to the best spots to admire the **Cathedral Bluffs** and the rest of the escarpment, a mere 5-minute drive further east. Quite a change of scenery, you'll see!

STROLL 13

Full loop:
7.5 km (2 hr)

Shorter version:
You could do the first part of the stroll, west of Fishleigh Drive in 3.6 km (55 min), or the section east of Scarboro Crescent in 1.6 km (25 min).

Game for more?
Drive to **Bluffer's Park**. (Take Scarboro Crescent or Midland Ave. back to Kingston Rd. Turn right on Kingston, then right on Brimley Rd. South into the park.) Drive to the last parking lot to your left. From there up to where the beach gets to its narrowest and back is 2.8 km (45 min).

Parking & TTC
• Bus line **#12** stops at **Rosetta McClain Gardens**.
• There's free parking at the **Gardens**.
• There's free street parking on Scarboro Crescent and adjacent streets around **Scarborough Bluffs Park**.

Other TIPS
• Dogs are not allowed in **Rosetta McClain Gardens**.

The Beach
To get to this stroll, I like to drive through **The Beach** on Queen Street East, and make a stop at **Remarkable Bean** (2242 Queen East) to grab a cup of coffee (and some of their amazing salty muffins).

Rosetta McClain Gardens is a 12-min drive further east, along Kingston Road.

The Gardens
1 From Kingston Road, you can access **Rosetta McClain Garden**'s parking lot, just before Glen Everest Road. You could tour the gardens in 15 minutes but there's a lot to be admired here.

The site is perched atop the cliffs so you'll be able to catch a breathtaking view of Lake Ontario, 60 metres below, as you take a turn along the trail.

In the centre, there are symmetrical raised planter beds adorned with a few large boulders.

2 On the eastern part of **Rosetta**, you'll find a mature and luscious forest (beautiful in the fall).

In the northeast corner of the park is an elegant vine-covered trellis near a rose garden.

3 Back towards the parking lot are some interesting ruins of an old farm. You can exit there and turn right on Glen Everest Road. Then take the closed road to your right (between the garden plots and Fishleigh Drive) to get down to the beach. Note that it is steep and can be slippery when wet.

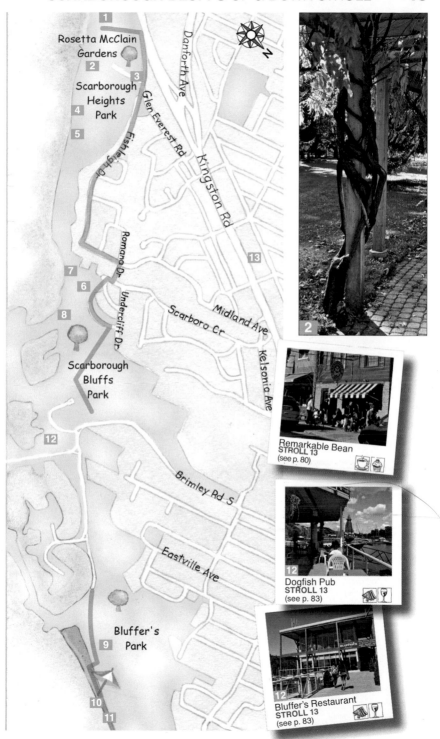

1

Rosetta McClain Gardens

2

3

Scarborough Heights Park

4

5

Danforth Ave

Glen Everest Rd

Fishleigh Dr

N

Kingston Rd

13

Romana Dr

7

6

Undercliff Dr

8

Scarboro Cr

Midland Ave

Kelsonia Ave

Scarborough Bluffs Park

12

Brimley Rd S

Eastville Ave

Bluffer's Park

9

10

11

Remarkable Bean
STROLL 13
(see p. 80)

12
Dogfish Pub
STROLL 13
(see p. 83)

12
Bluffer's Restaurant
STROLL 13
(see p. 83)

The Cathedral

4 The paved lane fades into a hard pressed dirt road following the shore.

Huge boulders were used to create a few breakwalls. Lovely tall grasses run up the hill.

5 In 10 minutes, you'll get a fantastic view of the white cliffs carved in such a way to have inspired the name **The Cathedral**.

The panorama is positively surreal, when you stop to consider that you're only a 30-min drive from downtown Toronto.

Scarboro Crescent

Back to Glen Everest Road, keep your right and follow Fishleigh. It will turn left into Midland Avenue. Take the first street right (Romana Drive), then turn right at Scarboro Crescent. You've arrived at **Scarborough Bluffs Park**. (Note that there's free parking along Scarboro Crescent and nearby streets.)

6 Entering the park at the foot of Scarboro Crescent, keep your right as you walk towards the lake and you'll reach the first of a series of benches, each offering a grand panoramic view. (Try them all!) Facing you, the lake spreads endlessly.

7 Looking to your right, you'll discover the **Bluffs**, covered with trees.

Looking down to your left, you'll see the 400 acres of **Bluffer's Park**, with its marina, meandering roads and more cliffs with rocky peaks.

8 On the park's eastern side (where the tennis courts are), there's an engaging path running through mature trees, which borders the cliffs further to your left.

Bluffer's Park

If you still have the energy after you've returned to your starting point, I strongly recommend you drive east to **Bluffer's Park** (at the foot of Brimley Road South).

9 The beach spreads east of the last parking lot to your left. You reach it via a trail at the base of the cliffs (which sit blazing under the sun and look amazing during the fall).

10 When the sand is dry, it is some of the finest I've seen in the Greater Toronto Aea. The beach, quite broad near the marina, narrows gradually.

11 Last time I visited, people had built a whimsical (and solid) shack out of driftwood in the last part of the beach.

12 The seasonal **Bluffer's Restaurant** is located at the foot of Brimley Road in the marina. It includes **Dogfish Pub**, offering lighter fare downstairs. (Both open daily at least from 11 a.m., April to October.)

The Murals

13 On your way back, try to spot the ten murals to be found left and right between Warden and Midland. Our favourites are the row boat approaching the cliffs at 2384 Kingston, and the marching band at 1577 Kingston.

SUNNYSIDE
ENDLESS STROLL
14

A stroll by glistening water

You can make this stroll as short or as long as you want, without ever loosing sight of the sparkly water of Lake Ontario. From **Sunnyside Pavilion**, it would take you an hour to reach the gorgeous gazebo, 3.5 km further west at the end of the promenade, or fifteen minutes to walk eastbound to **Easy Restaurant**, a popular all-day breakfast place by the walkway running across the Lake Shore, at the foot of Roncesvalles. In between, as a bonus: the quiet beat of the beach life, the white swans, the European-like courtyard of the pavilion, two lovely pedestrian bridges, a butterfly habitat, willow trees brushing the water, sculptures... and cute joggers.

STROLL 14

Full loop (west of Humber Bay Bridge):
5.7 km (1 hr 25 min)

Full loop (east of Humber Bay Bridge):
4.8 km (1 hr 10 min)

Shorter version:
The loop between the **Sunnyside Pavilion** and the **Humber Bay Arch Bridge** is 3.1 km long (45 min).

Game for more?
A .7 km waterfront trail now links the gazebo (see #2) to **Mimico Linear Park** near **Birds & Beans** (read #1)!

Parking & TTC
• The streetcar **#501** runs along Lake Shore.
• For the west loop, there are paid parking lots by Humber Bay Park Rd. (West and East). Or try your luck for $1/hr parking along Marine Parade Dr.
• For the east loop, arriving westbound from Lake Shore, keep your left, past Colborne Lodge Dr., to take the Lake Shore exit and drive through.
• Arriving eastbound from Lake Shore, turn right, past Ellis Ave., into the parking lot.

West loop stroll

1 If you want to grab a coffee before starting the west loop stroll, there's country-like **Birds & Beans Café** at 2413 Lake Shore Blvd. Many bird watchers like to meet there (I've even seen organized bird watching walks announced). And now that a trail links the café to **Humber Park**, .7 km further east, you might want to park near the café.

Or drive to the parking lot along Humber Bay Park Rd. West. On the west side of this road, you'll find the **Humber Bay Promenade**.

2 At the end of the .5 km promenade, there's a large gazebo overlooking the lake (the perfect spot to sip your coffee).

3 Along the way, you'll see a garden and the shiny sculpture *Sail Forms* by artist Bruce Garner, leaning over a reflecting pool.

Mimico Creek

4 Return towards the parking lot and cross the white pedestrian bridge going over **Mimico Creek**, which empties into Lake Ontario on your right.

5 Walk along Marine Parade Drive and enter the park when you see a sign for the **Humber Butterfly Habitat**. Its paths are lined with flowers appealing to butterflies, tall grasses and beautiful metal crows on poles. (Last time we visited, birds had chosen to build their nests in the hollow body of these crows.)

6 Follow the paved path towards the lake and you'll come across a surprising memorial.

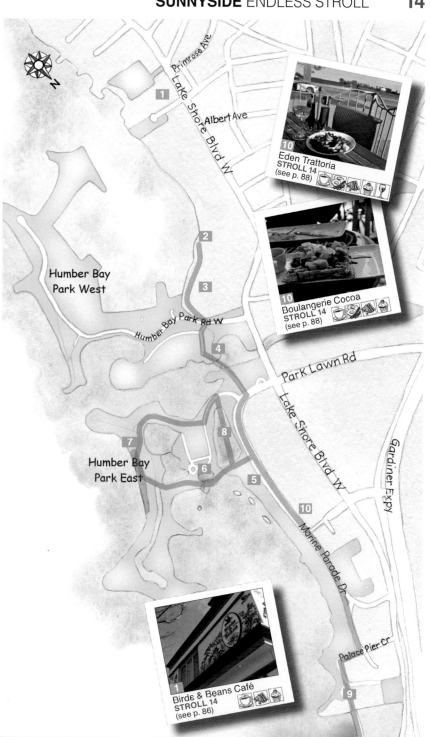

Eden Trattoria
STROLL 14
(see p. 88)

Boulangerie Cocoa
STROLL 14
(see p. 88)

Birds & Beans Café
STROLL 14
(see p. 86)

Humber Bay
Park West

Humber Bay
Park East

Primrose Ave

Lake Shore Blvd W

Albert Ave

Humber Bay Park Rd W

Park Lawn Rd

Lake Shore Blvd W

Marine Parade Dr

Gardiner Expy

Palace Pier Cr

The sundial of **Air India Memorial** was erected for the 329 victims of the Air India terrorist bombing in 1985.

7 Keep going until you reach the lake and turn right to find a pretty oasis where a small stream runs into the lake.

8 Then find your way through the parking lot and walk to your left until you see decking crossing basins. They serve to filter storm water. Chances are you'll see cranes and cormorants from this platform. And don't forget to look down into the water for gigantic fish!

Walk along the deck, then back to Marine Parade Drive where you'll turn right.

Humber Bay Bridge

Aim for **Humber Bay Bridge**, 1 km further east. On the way, you'll see another entrance to the pebble trail of the **Butterfly Habitat** (marked with an arch made of metal butterflies).

9 The pedestrian bridge is 139 metres long and you'll notice twenty turtles and four snakes carved into its structure.

10 On your way back to your starting point, you might want to stop at **Eden Trattoria** (58 Marine Parade Drive), for drinks or lunch. This waterfront restaurant has great bay windows with a view and a wonderful patio. (It is open daily at 8 a.m. for breakfast.)

Boulangerie Cocoa is hidden behind! Also open early, it serves **Starbucks** coffee and all-day brunch.

East loop stroll

11 The best parking lot to enjoy the east loop is just east of Ellis Avenue. The **Humber Bay Bridge** is about 1 km west of it, with **Sir Casimir Gzowski Park** in between.

Easy Restaurant
STROLL 14
(see p. 90)

Sunnyside Café
STROLL 14
(see p. 90)

Sunnyside Pavilion

12 Walking along **Sunnyside Beach**, east of the parking lot, you'll reach the great waterfront patio of seasonal **Sunnyside Pavilion Café** by the boardwalk (a good place to observe swans while having lunch (it usually opens at 11:30 a.m.).

Their courtyard is lovely, with flowers and a classic fountain. Don't miss the opportunity to admire the wonderful view from their second level if it is open.

13 Just east of the pavilion is the huge **Gus Ryder Public Pool**. As you stroll along the long turquoise rectangle of the pool, chances are you'll see the kite surfers' wings above the tree line.

Budapest Park

14 Keep walking east and you're in cute **Budapest Park** (with the perfect wading pool in the shade of tall trees). The beach side on your right is very pretty and less frequented than **Sunnyside Beach**.

15 A few more minutes further east and you'll reach the pedestrian bridge crossing over the Gardiner. Check out the view of the lake from this bridge!

16 If you want to push it a bit further, you'll find the popular all-day breakfast **Easy Restaurant** at the intersection of Roncesvalles Avenue and Queen Street West (1645 Queen West).

This laid-back place also serves lunch and dinner and gets busy on the weekends.

CABBAGETOWN
NOOKS & CRANNIES STROLL
15

Eye candy everywhere we look

This neighbourhood has a unique character. Stroll through its labyrinth of intimate dead-ends, secret lanes and narrow streets crowded with small Victorian houses, and you'll feel like you're in some "old world" village living at its own pace and following its own rules. You'll find little cottages fit to be by a lake off Wellesley Cottage Lane, great houses with **Wellesley Park** as a front yard, and a pathway made out of grave stones in **Necropolis**, one of Toronto's oldest cemeteries. There's so much to look at, you might forget the time and be late for dinner. (No problem, grab some great take-out at local **Daniel & Daniel** on your way.)

STROLL
15

Full loop:
5.6 km (1 hr 25 min)

Shorter version:
The best nooks and crannies are found along Wellesley St. East. You can park on Sumach north of Amelia St. and start the stroll going east on Amelia as described, up to the point where you reach Sackville St. (where you'll turn left instead of right, to reach Amelia and get back to your car). It's a 2-km stroll (30 min).

Game for more?
At the east end of Carlton, you'll see **Riverdale Park West**. It is part of the **Riverdale Sunset Stroll** (**Stroll 22**, p. 133).

Parking & TTC
• The streetcar **#506** runs along Parliament and Carlton.
• You're allowed to park for free on most streets east of Parliament Street.

Other TIPS
• There's a **Farmers' Market** at **Riverdale Farm** on Tuesdays, 3 p.m. to 7 p.m., mid-May to late October.

Spruce Street

1 I like to start this stroll at Spruce Street, especially in the morning (summer light at 8 a.m. is simply gorgeous in this luscious environment).

Walk east to see a section of Cabbagetown which you can't access by car. Take the path to your left at the end of Spruce.

2 Turn left onto Geneva Avenue for your first close look at Cabbagetown's little row houses. Then, turn right on Sumach Street, and right again into Gordon Sinclair Lane.

This lane is especially pretty in the fall.

Sumach Street

3 Keep going north then turn left at Carlton Street, and right on Sumach Street. You'll walk along **Riverdale Park** and will notice many beautiful houses on the way.

4 At Winchester, turn right to enter the **Necropolis Cemetery**, one of the oldest cemeteries in Toronto.

5 Follow the road to your right and walk straight, where it curves, until you reach Section R. To your left, you'll see the most bucolic scene: two stone trails lined with memorial plates, sheltered by the trees.

They will lead to the main loop and back to the entrance of the cemetery, where you'll turn right to get to Sumach Street.

Stroll ahead to Amelia Street, then turn right to access a little gem of a park hidden from the street: **Wellesley Park**.

Wellesley Park

6 You'll see many houses facing this park on
the south side. No street,
no sidewalk. Hilly **Wellesley Park** is their front yard.
That's something else, isn't
it? A winding path runs
through the park.

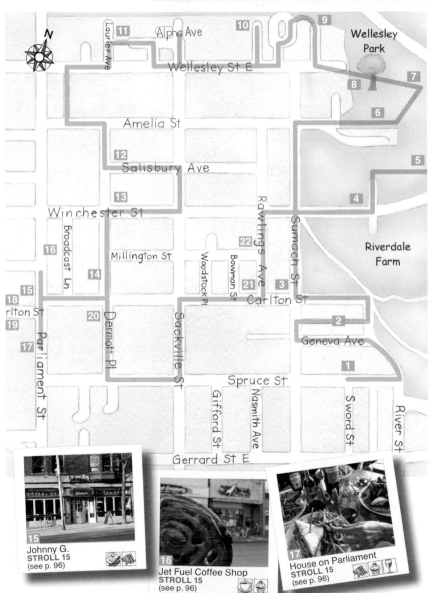

Johnny G.
STROLL 15
(see p. 96)

Jet Fuel Coffee Shop
STROLL 15
(see p. 96)

House on Parliament
STROLL 15
(see p. 96)

7 There's a long stair-case in the northeast corner. It leads to Rose-dale Valley Road (which is another stroll in itself).

8 Stay in the park and follow the path up the northwest corner to Welles-ley Street East.

Wellesley Street

Every road going north from Wellesley Street East is worth visiting! Most of them are dead-end streets, some with little dirt paths to access the next.

9 Turn right on Parkview Avenue and walk to the end. You'll find a dirt road going left to reach St. James Court running around a small block. (Note that there are some pub-lic parking spots along the wall just off the little road.)

10 Off St. James Court, turn right, then right again onto Wellesley Ave-nue. This dead-end street is special. It ends with a touching plate erected in memory of a fellow resi-dent who died in the 90s. (A very nice man who lives on that street told me about this neighbour.)

The next road west is Sackville Street. Walk to the end and look into the cute Alpha Avenue to your left. Then return to Wellesley Street and turn right into Wellesley Cottage.

11 Turn left to see the little cottages, so cute they look like doll houses. You can then walk west through a small dirt path to access Laurier Avenue. Back on Wellesley Street, turn right, then take Iro-quois Lane to your left.

CABBAGETOWN NOOKS & CRANNIES STROLL

At the corner of Iroquois Lane and Amelia Street (12 Amelia Street), the very popular Italian restaurant **F'Amelia** everyone is raving about, has opened for dinner and weekend brunch. (The place has a lovely outdoor patio.)

Salisbury Avenue

12 Walk east on Amelia, then turn right at Metcalfe Street to Salisbury Avenue. This street on your left is truly lovely. The large house on the corner at its entrance is impressive.

There's a cosy feeling to the rest of the street (especially in December when Christmas lights are up). If you're doing the short version of the stroll, turn left at Sackville Street. Otherwise, turn right, then right again at Winchester Street.

Winchester Street

13 Soon, you'll walk by the majestic **Toronto Dance Theatre** (a former church).

14 Turn left at Metcalfe Street and look up to see all kinds of interesting architectural detail.

Then take Carlton to your right to reach Parliament for a bit of fun window shopping and to have a bite, a coffee, or a drink. (Don't worry, I'll make you return to this unique section of Cabbagetown at the end of the stroll!)

Carlton Street

15 If you're in the mood for a substantial breakfast, try **Johnny G.** across the street (478 Parliament).

16 If you're just craving a great coffee, **Jet Fuel** further north on the east side (519 Parliament) is a must. Their foamy lattes are delicious, and if you show up before 11 a.m., they will still have a few tasty pastries to offer.

17 If you'd rather sit for lunch, try charming bistro **House on Parliament**, south of Carlton (454 Parliament). Their cute patio is lovely on a hot sunny day.

18 **Daniel & Daniel**, at 248 Carlton, sells gourmet take-out options.

You've got to make a stop at **Labour of Love** at 242 Carlton. This shop has put together a fantastic assortment of accessories (and cards). I fell in love with their jewelry selection.

19 Across the street is **Kendall & Co.**, the brilliant shop run by Kendall Williams and his team of residential designers (227 Carlton). Their Rug Collection is to die for (but I'd rather live with it).

Nearby **Stout Irish Pub** at 221 Carlton is prettier and bigger inside than one would expect.

20 Go back to Carlton Street east of Parliament and turn right through Dermott Place, for a true small town feel.

21 Turn left on Spruce, left again on Sackville, and right on Carlton to see one last lane: Rawlings Avenue. It is set between two gorgeous ivy-covered houses.

22 Walk north on Rawlings, turn right on Winchester to Sumach and cross **Riverdale Park** to stroll's starting point.

Colourful and junky mix

OK, this is not exactly a stroll to burn off calories. You'll want to stop every ten metres to explore it all. Here, old bargain stores mingle with slick urban boutiques, carnivores and vegetarians mix peacefully, vintage shops sit next to bulk ethnic markets. Colourful murals and graffiti add to the charm. There truly is a special vibe to this high-density neighbourhood offering a unique combo of residential and commercial. You could spend a whole day browsing, eating and drinking in this funky little block... with Chinatown as a bonus.

STROLL
16

Full loop:
2.1 km (30 min)

Shorter version:
Between the two of them, cool Augusta and funky Kensington Avenues (with a bit of Baldwin Street in the middle), you get the full spirit of **Kensington Market** in a 1.4 km stroll (20 min).

Game for more?
The **Queen Street Smart Stroll** (**Stroll 4**, p. 29) is a 5-min walk south of this stroll.

Parking & TTC
• The streetcar **#506** runs along College.
• You might be lucky and find a spot on Augusta. I like the parking lot on Bellevue Ave. south of Nassau to start in this part of the stroll but there's a much cheaper **Green P** on Baldwin, east of Kensington Avenue.

Other TIPS
• Street celebrations are really this neighbourhood's forte (think Kensington Winter Solstice Parade). See **www.pskensington. ca** to see if they're still offring their inspiring **Pedestrian Sundays**.

Denison Square

1 Walk south on Bellevue Avenue and you'll arrive at **Denison Square**. I was seduced by the life-size statue of Al Waxman (Canadian actor and director) casually looking over the benches in the northeast corner.

Turn left into the park to get to Augusta, which you'll want to explore all the way up to College.

Augusta Street

This is a street where **Urban Herbivore** sits near a **Big Fat Burrito**, a sushi bar stands by an espresso bar, not too far from a **Hungary Thaï** (get it?) and **Jumbo Empanadas**.

2 We tried and loved **The Grilled Cheese** restaurant at 66 1/2 Nassau Street.

Further west on Nassau, you'll find all-day breakfast **KOS Restaurant** at the corner of Nassau and Bellevue, with full bar and a huge patio. It is facing cool **Lettuce Knit**.

3 North of Augusta, we enjoyed browsing through the cool spread at the gift shop **Good Egg** (267 Augusta).

Neighbour **Bungalow** (273) is a trendy fashion store including a large vintage section. (They opened **Bungalow West** across the street at 244.)

4 **Blue Banana Market** (250) is a marketplace which feels like a souk (opens at 11 a.m.).

5 Not to be confused with **Super Market** (268) the cool restauran venue serving tasty tapas

KENSINGTON TRULY ECLECTIC STROLL

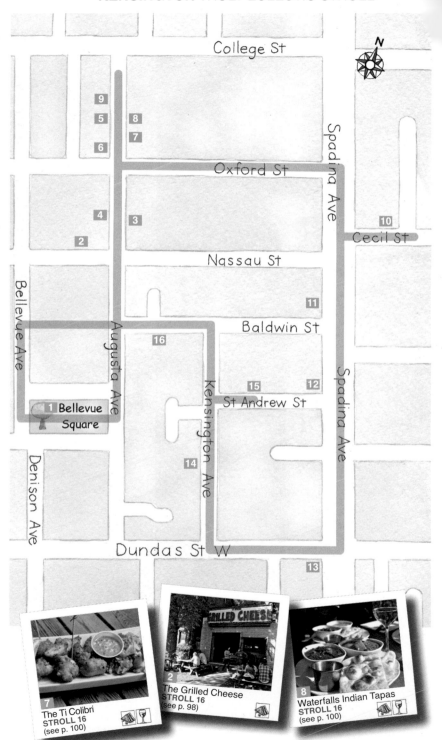

N

College St

9
5 8
6 7

Oxford St

Spadina Ave

4
3
2

10

Cecil St

Bellevue Ave

Nassau St

11

Augusta Ave

Baldwin St

16

15 12

Spadina Ave

1 Bellevue Square

St Andrew St

Kensington Ave

14

Denison Ave

Dundas St W

13

7
The Ti Colibri
STROLL 16
(see p. 100)

2
The Grilled Cheese
STROLL 16
(see p. 98)

8
Waterfalls Indian Tapas
STROLL 16
(see p. 100)

6 Past Oxford Street, there's the airy restaurant **Urban Herbivore** facing **Wanda's Pie in the Sky** (where I've had a few tasty salads... and some good pie).

7 Next time I do this stroll, I'll eat in the lovely (and secluded) back patio with Caribbean vibe of **The Ti Colibri** (291 Augusta). The vegetarian restaurant was waiting for its liquor license at the time of print (a Ti'Punch under the casa would be devine).

8 We've had delicious Indian tapas at **Waterfalls Indian Tapas** (303).Their outdoor patio is the place to have a drink and people watch at the end of a sunny afternoon (when a sparkling mojito in a highball glass looks, and tastes, at its best).

9 Further north, I love to check **Fresh Collective**'s selection of local designers (274).

Spadina Avenue

Chinatown is at the edge of **Kensington Market** along Spadina and Dundas.

The restaurants, stalls and stores are of a different nature and they offer an exotic complement to the **Market**'s eclectic blocks.

The densely aligned signage is mainly Chinese or Vietnamese (I think...). Most passersby are of Asian descent. It's like travelling, without paying for a plane ticket!

Arriving from Oxford Street, across Spadina you'll find **Mother's Dumplings** (421 Spadina, no of Cecil Street).

Regulars brought me to this pretty and affordable place specializing in dumplings. I found it less crowded than many of the popular restaurants closer to Dundas.

10 Walking south, turn left on Cecil Street, where you can't miss **Sonic**'s funky facade! This tiny coffee shop with patio serves alcohol.

11 My favourite places nearby to peruse for bargains (or merchandise I don't see anywhere else) are: **Harvest Int'l Trading** (406 Spadina Avenue), **B & J Trading** (376) and **Tap Phong Trading Co.** (360, south of Baldwin St.).

12 On both sides of St. Andrew at Spadina are to two fun restaurants: **Gold Diamond Chinese Restaurant**, a large banquet-like room on the second floor of 346 Spadina serving a wide selection of dim sum on rolling carts, and Vietnamese **Pho Hung** across the street.

13 As you approach Dundas Street, you can see the cooks at work through the restaurants' windows, the exotic offerings on the outdoor stalls, and long red dragons perched on tall poles.

For a great panorama of **Chinatown**, you can take the elevator to reach the **Sky Dragon Restaurant** (on the 4th floor of **Dragon City** at 280 Spadina). It is flanked with a long balcony looking east.

This small shopping mall also is home to a genuine karaoke bar with private booths: **Echo** (also on the second floor).

Kensington Avenue

14 Turn right at Dundas Street, then right again onto Kensington Avenue. Most of the stretch of this street is chock-full of funky vintage clothing stores.

If you were a teen in the 70's, chances are you'll recognize most of the stuff in these shops...

You don't need to be a fan of vintage clothes to be charmed by the candy coloured facades on the street and the whimsical clothes inside the likes of: **Exile**, **Flashback**, **Courage My Love** or **Dancing Days**, to name a few.

15 Just east on St. Andrews is another fun place to investigate: **Moonbeam Coffee**. The narrow café/restaurant is quite long with front and back patios.

Baldwin Street

16 Baldwin Street comes next. It is in the heart of the market. At **Chocolate Addict** (185 Baldwin), there was a sign stating: "I could give up chocolate but I'm not a quitter".

At the end of the street chills **Roach-O- Rama**, bragging they've served potheads since ah... they forget. (There's a theme right here, isn't there?)

The best of the rest includes bakeries, cheese store, nut importers, fruit and vegetable stalls, bargain stores and other places to discover as you stroll around.

Jimmy's Coffee recently opened (at 191) with an industrial lounge and a fantastic back patio.

Like strolling through a magazine

Think glossy lifestyle magazine and you get the picture. It seems that over 80% of the shops in this part of town are home decor related, which is already an attraction in itself. But the architecture of the surrounding stone buildings makes it even more interesting. Nearby **George Brown College** and **St. Lawrence Market** keep the area busy. Cafés and little restaurants provide perfect breaks for girlfriends to digest all the great decorating ideas they've gathered. The stores range from the vintage shop to the boutique with ultra slick high-end Italian furniture sold at the cost of a small car. Hey! One can always dream...

STROLL 17

Full loop:
3.6 km (55 min)

Shorter version:
You'll find most of the home decor stores on King and Adelaide between Jarvis and Parliament, a 2.2 km stroll (35 min).

Game for more?
The Distillery Red Brick Stroll
(**Stroll 7**, p. 43) is just a few minutes south of this stroll.

Parking & TTC
• The streetcar **#504** runs along King and **#501** along Queen.
• There is a large parking lot accessible off Parliament, south of Front Street.
• There's a cheaper parking lot at the corner of The Esplanade and Berkeley Street (accessible from Front Street).

Other TIPS
• It's better not to do this stroll on Mondays, when many stores are closed.
• Check the calendar of events in **www.thedistillerydistrict.com** for a listing of year-round events at **The Distillery**.

Gilead Place
The problem with street parking around this stroll is the time limit they impose.

If you want to avoid the stress of having to rush back to your car in the middle of the stroll, I recommend you go to the parking lot just east of Parliament, on Mill Street.

Walk north on Trinity Street and go straight to King Street East, where you'll turn right. This part of King East includes two very good options for early breakfast (a girl needs nourishment before undertaking serious window shopping, doesn't she?).

1 The cute breakfast place **Morning Glory** at 457 King East, just east of Gilead Place, serves very good food. Closed Tuesday and Wednesday, open rest of the weekdays 8:30 a.m. to 3 p.m. and 9 a.m. to 3 p.m on weekends.

2 **Gilead Café** is right around the corner (4 Gilead Place). It is part of **Jamie Kennedy Kitchens**. They offer tasty breakfast and lunch in a sunny decor (open 8 a.m. to 3 p.m., except Sundays when it opens at 10 a.m.).

3 Your first stop should be at high-end furniture store **Studio b** on King across from **Morning Glory** (opens at 9:30 a.m. on weekdays, 11 a.m. on Saturdays, closed on Sundays).

4 Then walk south on Gilead Place and turn right on Eastern Avenue to visit **Fresh Home & Garden** (16 Eastern).

It is filled with dreamy garden furniture and outdoor decor items (open 10 a.m. to 5 p.m., opens at 12 noon on Sundays).

King Street East

Then, from Eastern, turn right at Trinity Street. (At the time of print there were signs announcing that **Tandem Café** would open soon across from Trinity, at 368 King East).

Gilead Café
STROLL 17
(see p. 104)

Le Petit Déjeuner
STROLL 17
(see p. 107)

Pacific Junction Hotel
STROLL 17
(see p. 106)

On King Street, walk west to Parliament. Past Parliament, awaits a line-up of high-end and edgy stores.

5 **Klaus** (300 King East) is so hip it feels like a modern museum. Need a life-size horse lamp? This is your place. (They always feature dramatic lamps in their striking window.)

Kiosk (288) is equally avant-garde but the ambiance is more sobering. (Some people do have the money to buy an $ 8,000 Italian outdoor ottoman.)

The full glass facade of **Bulthaup** (280) reveals all the ultra slick designs of their dream kitchens (including an innovative foldable one).

6 When you're ready for a bowl of mojito and some alligator, you've got to consider most whimsical island-themed **Pacific Junction Hotel** (234).

7 Luxurious **Trianon** (247) features truly exquisite creations using branches and feathers.

South of it, at 44 Sherbourne, awaits breezy **Jardin de Ville 1956**, filled with dreamy terrace concepts.

8 Back on King, landmark bookstore/gallery **D & E Lake** is not to be missed (239) if you're a collector of rare books, maps or prints.

Looking for a unique book for a special person? Speak with the very resourcefull owner.

Stacaro (225, just after **UrbanAmish Interiors**) offers a vast collection of masculine design throughout its connecting rooms.

9 While you are on this part of King, I must point out **Le Petit Déjeuner** (191 King East), a Belgian restaurant offering delicious all-day breakfast, lunch and dinner menus.

10 The next showroom which thrilled us was **Modern Weave** (160 King East). You'll think this is an art gallery. And it gets better inside. At the back, each rug is a piece of art.

Jarvis Street

11 If you walk past Jarvis Street, you'll reach picturesque **St. James Park**, followed by **St. James Cathedral**, with the best stained-glass windows tryptic in town. (By the way, free recitals are held in the cathedral on Tuesdays at 1 p.m., September to June.) It faces **Toronto Sculpture Garden**.

12 Look up over the southwest corner at Jarvis and King to admire the Corinthian columns and elegant cupola of **St. Lawrence Hall** over the heritage buildings.

13 Then, it's back to the design stroll by turning north on Jarvis. In **Ma Zone** (63 Jarvis Street), you'll find an abundance of home decor and gift ideas.

At the corner of Adelaide and Jarvis is pretty **G for Gelato** (serving gelato, café and light lunches).

14 Across the street is gorgeous **Bo Concept** with urban Danish design (and great reclaimed wood).

Next to it, **Gautier** presents French furniture (including lots of clever storage concepts).

Keep walking east on Adelaide.

15 **Resource Furniture** (366 Adelaide E.) specializes in ingenious double-duty systems turning living rooms and offices into guest rooms.

Berkeley Street

From Adelaide, turn left on Berkeley Street. You'll pass by **Alumnae Theatre**.

16 **Berkeley Café** at 141 Berkeley is a small Victorian-inspired restaurant with character and a cute patio (open weekdays only 9 a.m. to 3 p.m.).

17 **Berkeley Church**, to your left on Queen, is part of an intriguing venue.

Queen Street

18 On Queen, walk east to get to a Toronto fixture: **Marty Millionaire** (345 Queen E.). You never know what to expect amidst their most eclectic selection of furniture: a life-size Indian chief, an Egyptian god...

19 **Adornments on Queen**, a quaint store packed with home accessories at 338, includes **Steeped and Infused**.

Parliament Street

20 Turn right on Parliament and at Adelaide, you'll find the entrance to **Andrew Richard Designs**, the fine outdoor furniture department within **UpCountry**.

For a big finish, walk across the street into **Roche Bobois** (101 Parliament) to admire modern high-end design.

KING WEST
TRENDY STROLL
18

Build it and they will come

We can complain all we want about the condos popping up all over downtown but when they're built in a
great location such as King West, with all its architectural detail, it injects the life required to attract all kinds
of businesses. The **Thompson Hotel** has set the tone
for a more trendy feeling (with a superb lounge and a
patio by an outdoor reflecting pool at street level). The
Drake General Store followed. Then there's the cool
decor of **Marben**, the exotic **Spice Route**, **Brassaii**'s
gorgeous courtyard, the cushion-filled **Atelier Café
Lounge**, the inspiring hardware store **Lee Valley** and
more home decor stores and restaurants, with great
coffee shops, at both ends of this urban stroll.

STROLL
18

Full loop:
2.5 km (40 min)

Shorter version:
You can cut this stroll to 1.5 km (25 min) by walking straight to the **Thompson Hotel** and crossing to Stewart St., then turning right to reach Portland. On King West, cut through the courtyard of **Rodney's Oyster Bar** to return to Wellington.

Game for more?
Queen Street Smart Stroll (**Stroll 4**, p. 29) is a 5-min walk north of this stroll. **Downtown Courtyards Stroll** (**Stroll 1**, p. 13) is 5 min east of this stroll.

Parking & TTC
• The streetcar **#504** runs along King.
• The indoor parking lot on the west side of Portland Street (north of Front), is cheaper than the street parking.

Other TIPS
• If you catch an early dinner after the stroll, you could then head to the **TIFF Bell Lightbox** for a movie. It is located at 350 King W., a 5-min. walk east of Spadina.

Niagara Street
1   Park in the **Portland Park Village** parking lot off Portland, just north of Front Street. Then exit from the north pedestrian path going through the town houses and condos. You'll walk under a curious town house which looks like it is suspended in the air, to access Niagara Street and the park.

2   **Victoria Memorial Park** was a military burial ground from 1793 to 1863, for the people involved with **Fort York**. So, the park now stands above some 400 graves! Abandoned and vandalized in the 1880s, only 17 gravestones were preserved.

3   Keep walking west on Niagara and you'll see **Thor Espresso Bar** (35 Bathurst). The Iceland-inspired café is clad in icy whites and blond wood, with woolly furs on the chairs in the winter.

Bathurst Street
4   Turn right on Bathurst and right again to reach **Thompson Toronto Hotel** (550 Wellington West). It is a must, to have a look at their amazing dark lounge, quite dramatic with the huge mural by Barcelonian artist Javier Marisca of a Toronto cityscape.

5   We had a $15 drink there to better admire it, but I think next time, I would rather have a cocktail on the outdoor patio of nearby stylish **Scarpetta**. It sits by a lovely reflecting pool. You can then walk north through a corridor leading to Stewart Street.

6 On Stewart, look to your right to see the cluster of towering luxury condos. Then turn left to Bathurst Street and you'll be facing **Drake General Store** (82A Bathurst). This fun gift shop is filled with unusual gadgets.

I did not expect to find such a selection of funky clothes amidst the more classic ones in **Freda's** (86 Bathurst). Visit **www.fredas.com** to get an idea of the collections in this high-end boutique.

7 The vast bakery **Brioche Dorée** recently opened at 650 King W. with a wide spread of sweet and salty pastries.

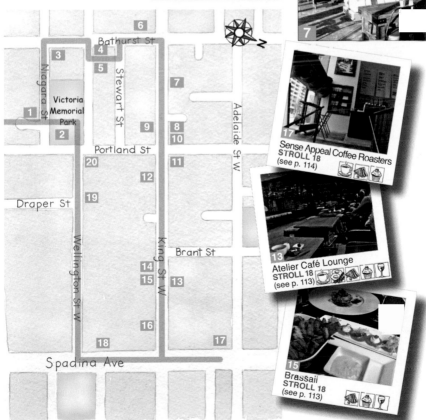

17 Sense Appeal Coffee Roasters
STROLL 18
(see p. 114)

13 Atelier Café Lounge
STROLL 18
(see p. 113)

15 Brassaii
STROLL 18
(see p. 113)

King Street West

8 From then on, this stroll will feel like a gourmet tour. The area is packed with all kinds of restaurants and patios. I'm no expert and have not tried them all, but I want to point out those with distinct features which caught my attention, starting with the carved garage door of chic nightclub **Cheval** at 606 King West. ("Cheval" means horse in French. Look carefully and you'll distinguish them.)

9 Across the street is **Lee Lounge** (601 King West), with an emphasis on tapas to share, less expensive than famous chef Lee Susur's former restaurant. They are open at 5:30 p.m., Monday to Saturday.

I tried their most popular dish, the intriguing slaw salad. Let the waiter explain to you how to eat it!

10 Have you heard about a superb steam room in the area? It is found in the **Hamman Spa** (602 King West). On their website, I could see that the interior of the spa is as gorgeous as the pattern of metal curls on their building.

I did not dare try it because I had heard I'd have to sit fully naked with strangers... Not true! It turns out you have to wrap yourself in a towel, and the steam room is actually co-ed! (A fact which shouldn't be too intimidating if you go with many girlfriends.) Admission to the turkish steam room is $55 but it is complimentary with any treatment over $100.

11 Across Portland Street at 600 King West, **Bier Markt** (no "e") offers $25 beer tasting trays which would be great fun to share with friends.

12 On the south side of King are a series of small restorants serving tasty fast food specialties. **The One That Got Away** (581 King West) prepares delicious fish and chips. They offer sandwiches, salads and wraps made from a wide variety of fish.

Next door **Big Smoke Burger** gets great reviews.

Facing them is classy **Lee Valley** (590). If there's a hardware store that could appeal to girlfriends, this is the one! Ask for their catalogues.

13 **Atelier Café Lounge** (510) is easy to miss but you've got to admire this exotic lounge filled with cushions (and its spectacular restroom). It is open from 8 a.m., Monday to Friday, and 9 a.m. on Saturday, and serves good coffee, pastries and light lunch.

Patagonia opened further east (500). The outdoor clothing and gear boutique includes trendy casual wear.

14 It's facing the exotic restaurant **Spice Route** with a unique decor (499) serving fusion tapas from 4:30 p.m on weekdays and 5 p.m. on weekends, closed on Mondays.

15 **Brassaii** (461) includes a real gem of a patio hidden in the back of the courtyard, past **Firkin on King**.

It opens at 11:30 a.m. on weekdays and 10 a.m. on weekends.

16 Decadent **Soma Chocolatemaker** opened at 443 King West, just in time for me to include it in this stroll. You'll find a few tables in the back of the gorgeous old building.

It is followed by huge **Design Within Reach** furniture store and **Calphalon Culinary Center**, offering cooking classes and high-end kitchen supplies.

Spadina Avenue

17 On your left on Spadina, is **Sense Appeal Coffee Roasters** (96 Spadina), a serious coffee shop selling delicious food. **18** Going southbound on Spadina, you'll notice a fun little house which looks like it's fighting the big condos (64 Spadina). It used to be a home decor boutique. I hope it doesn't get torn down after all. It's too cute!

Big It Up (58 Spadina) sells all kinds of hats. They both face **Winners**.

Wellington West

Right, at 432 Wellington West, **Le Sélect Bistro** is the closest you can get to "ze reel ting" in Toronto. You'll pay the price but a visit to this French restaurant is still cheaper than a trip to Paris! **19** At **Marben** (488 Wellington West), you'll also feel at the top of the food chain, at a fraction of the cost. I love their decor with undulating birch.

20 Further, is the more conventional **Bar Wellington** (with good prices, and two patios).

Both places open at 11 a.m. Tuesday to Friday, and at 10 a.m. on weekends.

Follow the trail of local passions

The vitality of creativity in this part of town is palpable. Here, Queen Street is lined with the independent businesses of proud owners who followed their passions. Designers are selling their collections in their own small shops; savvy buyers offer their unique selection of specialty merchandise of all kinds (vintage or new); chefs open little restaurants; free spirits launch cafés where the self-employed and hip moms with babies attached mingle. **Ceili Cottage**, the local Irish pub, once built a tiny curling rink for its customers in the winter. I even know of an actress who opened her own little 50-seat theatre (**Red Sandcastle Theatre**) near icon gelato place **Ed's Real Scoop**. Can't get cooler than that!

STROLL 19

Full loop:
4.2 km (65 min)

Shorter version:
If you go from Booth to Jones Avenue and back, it will be a 1.8 km loop (30 min) in the heart of Leslieville.

Game for more?
The **Riverside Up & Coming Stroll** (**Stroll 23**, p. 139) starts where **Stroll 19** stops, west of **Jimmie Simpson Park**.

Parking & TTC
• The streetcar **#501** runs along Queen.
• You can easily find free street parking after 10 a.m. on the streets north and south of Queen East.

Other TIPS
• Many shops only open at 11 a.m. and are closed on Mondays.
• The **Farmers' Market** in **Jonathan Ashbridge Park**, east of Woodfield Road, is quite lively (Sundays, 9 a.m. to 2 p.m., end of May to end of October).
• The **Beach Cinema** (east of this stroll, past Coxwell) has comfortable seats and a large lounge with bay windows.

Logan Avenue

1 Leslieville starts at **Joy Bistro Bar** with its long patio overlooking **Jimmie Simpson Park** at the corner of Booth Avenue and Queen. They also feature an alluring courtyard on their east side (a great spot for a drink at the end of an afternoon stroll).

Lady Marmalade is located at 898 Queen East. It opens daily from 8 a.m. to at least 3 p.m. (cash only). Show up before 9 a.m. on weekends and skip weekdays between 11:30 a.m. and 1:30 p.m. if you want to avoid line-ups.

2 Within two blocks east of **Joy** are found all the good suppliers that can fill a foodie's pantry: colourfull fish store **Hooked**, charming **Leslieville Cheese Market**, comforting **Brick Street Bakery**, elegant **Rowe Farm**, retro **Paulette's**, proud **Mercury Espresso Bar** and cheerful **Ed's Real Scoop** gelato shop.

3 Businesses such as the small 50-seat (with a big line-up of shows) **Red Sandcastle Theatre** (922), **Swirl Wine Bar** (upstairs at 946) serving food in tiny Mason jars, and **Tizz** (952) with great affordable glam from local designer Tisiano Giusti, add to the area's cool factor.

4 Make the detour to see the huge mural on Dundas east of Logan. It is part of the international *Giant Storybook Project* (look them up on Facebook). It is located across from **Red Rocket Coffee**, a café within a flower shop.

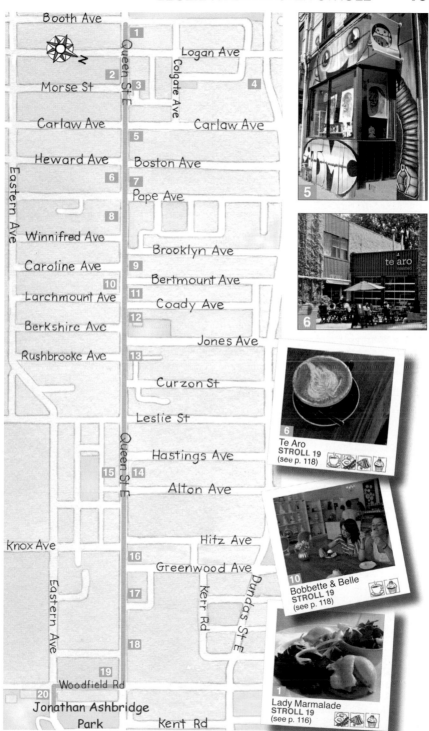

Te Aro
STROLL 19
(see p. 118)

Bobbette & Belle
STROLL 19
(see p. 118)

Lady Marmalade
STROLL 19
(see p. 116)

5 Past toy store/gallery **Atomic Toybot** (978), there are six great furniture stores between Carlaw and Bertmount, starting with **Zenpodium**, next to **MachineAge Modern** at 1000 Queen Street East.

6 Trendy **Baby on the Hip** and coffee roastery **Te Aro** at 983 Queen East (a French industrial café with a communal table and a vast patio) sit next to **Zig Zag**.

7 West of Pape is **Max's Wholesale** (1044), carrier of the whimsical Spanish line Desiguales!

8 East of Pape is the original designer store **Nathalie-Roze & Co.** (1015).

You'll find **Holy Cow!** (filled with huge and unusual items) further on the north side (1100).

9 It is succeeded by a cluster of interesting shops: **Pied-à-Terre** (within **Arts Market**), vintage furniture store **Bronze** and fashion store **Doll Factory by Damzels**.

From 9 a.m. to 4 p.m., there's all-day breakfast **OK OK Diner** (1128) adorned with a streetcar mural. From 5:30 p.m. to 7 p.m., it's **Goods and Provisions** (1124) with half-price drinks... and oysters!

Bertmount Avenue

10 Facing Bertmount is elegant **Bobbette and Belle** (1121). They make some of Toronto's best macarons and cupcakes and scones with fresh cream... which you can enjoy while admiring their exquisite cakes.

Next door, **Lil' Bean n' Green** offers an adorable place for parents to enjoy their coffee while their little ones play in the cute indoor playground in the back of the café.

Then there's **Hanoi 3 Seasons** (1135), a Vietnamese restaurant serving excellent and affordable cuisine (cash only).

11 Near Coady Ave. is **Guff**, with great vintage teak furniture (1142).

12 And one block further east is a local fixture: laid-back **Tango Palace Coffee Company** (1156).

13 In the next bundle of stores are **Purple Purl** (1162) the cool yarn shop, **Thrill of the Find** (1172) featuring second hand designer clothes, and **Studio We!** (1184) with edgy men's and women's clothing.

Across the street, don't miss two other interesting shops: home decor store **Cry if I want to** (1175) and fashion boutique **Dorly** (1173).

14 If you're into vintage clothing, **Gadabout** is for you (1300, past Hastings). It is bursting at the seams with great finds over two floors. Their second floor is filled with coats.

15 **Ceili Cottage**, across the street, is one-of-a-kind. It opens at 5 p.m. on weekdays and 12 noon on weekends and is one of our favourite places to have a beer. The inside is truly rustic, with thick walls and beams.

In the summer they have a large outdoor patio (where they installed a yurt last winter!)

16 East of Hilz Ave., **Flik by design** (1360 Queen E.) is the love child of the talented interior designer behind the decor of **Bobbette and Belle** and **The Pie Shack**.

It sits next to chic industrial vintage store **Love the Design**. (The owner's photographic art can be found in many Toronto restaurants.)

17 Further east is **Any Direct Flight** (1382), a stylish designer store combining fashion with coffee thanks to the **Flight Café** (also serving warm sandwiches).

If you are feeling adventurous, try Serbian **Rakia Bar** (1402), a unique brandy bar serving lunch and dinner in a slick urban decor a few steps down from street level. It includes a large side patio.

Woodfield Road

18 Before you reach Woodfield Road, you'll notice the historic home of the **Ashbridge Estate** built in 1854. (Public is allowed to stroll around the house.)

19 At the corner of Woodfield and Queen, you've got to visit the very cool **Up to You** (1483, entrance on Woodfield). It offers the most eclectic assortment of products laid out throughout a real apartment.

20 Keep going south, then turn left on Eastern to **Le Papillon on the Park** (1001 Eastern). In the summer, we can enjoy their outdoor balcony (closed Mondays and Tuesdays).

LIBERTY VILLAGE
FACTORY STROLL
20

So, what's the fuss all about?

Well, since 2005, the former industrial buildings have undergone some of the best conversions in town. Hip condos for young professionals have surrounded the area. Many restaurants (and a few shops) have followed, after a slow start. Interesting details to be observed abound. There's a canopied walkway reproducing the intimate feeling of similar public spaces in Italy and Spain, a gorgeous rug mural (where there used to be a carpet factory), huge roots climbing up old offices... and some hidden restaurants for those who venture away from the crowd.

STROLL
20

Full loop:
2.9 km (45 min)

Shorter version:
Cut the part of the stroll east of Hanna Avenue and you get a 2 km stroll (30 min).

Game for more?
The **Trinity-Bell-woods Artsy Stroll** (**Stroll 24**, p. 143) is only 10 minutes away. (Walk north on Dufferin St. to reach Queen.)

Parking & TTC
• The streetcar **#504** runs along King West.
• There's a large central parking lot on East Liberty St. between Hanna and Atlantic.
• If you're feeling lucky, try to get a spot in the cheaper parking lot just north of East Liberty St., and west of Atlantic or free street parking east of Hanna.

Other TIPS
• The Liberty Village farmers' market (called **Liberty Village MyMarket**) is open in the parking lot by East Liberty Street and Hanna Avenue, every Sunday from 9 a.m. to 2 p.m., from early June to end of October.

East Liberty Street

1 From the large parking lot on East Liberty Street (between Hanna and Atlantic), you can see the Liberty Market sign topping the long building, east of Hanna. Walk along that building and through the passage under the black cage-like structure. It will lead you to the canopied alley, a unique feature at **Liberty Village**.

2 I have seen a similar street treatment in Spain and was thrilled to find one in Toronto. There aren't enough little shops along the alley to fully recreate the European feeling but it's still exotic enough for us to enjoy.

3 I admired the creations at **For The Love of Cake** and salivated over $30 shoes... made out of chocolate at **The Golden Apple**. I checked a few clothing stores and sneaked into the dark and modern decor of sushi spot **Raaw Japanese Cuisine**.

At the end of the alley, you'll see the huge furniture store **Casalife** on your right. (**Liberty Village** now also includes **EQ3** at 51 Hanna.)

4 On your left is the Irish pub **Brazen Head,** with a fantastic patio on the second floor (perfect for a late afternoon drink during the summer).

5 Walk along East Liberty Street to get to **Liberty Village Park**, which recently acquired the huge *Perpetual Motion* sculpture, a creation of Chilean artist Francisco Gazitua (also read about his *Barca Volante* on p. 27).

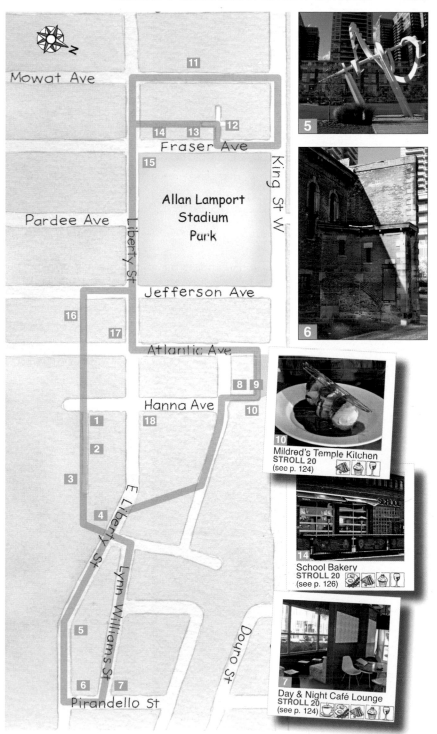

Mowat Ave

11

Fraser Ave

14 13 12

15

Allan Lamport Stadium Park

King St W

Pardee Ave

Liberty St

Jefferson Ave

16

17

Atlantic Ave

8 9

Hanna Ave 10

1

18

2

3

4

E Liberty St

Lynn Williams St

5

Douro St

6 7

Pirandello St

10 Mildred's Temple Kitchen
STROLL 20
(see p. 124)

14 School Bakery
STROLL 20
(see p. 126)

7 Day & Night Café Lounge
STROLL 20
(see p. 124)

6 There's a peculiar heritage building in the park. Walk around to view it from Pirandello Street. (It provides the best angle to admire the mix of old and new which characterizes **Liberty Village**.)

7 Across the street, **Day & Night Café Lounge** opens at 7:30 a.m. on weekays and 8 a.m. on weekends. I liked its breezy decor. Haven't tried their food but they have a wide menu to choose from.

Next, turn left into Lynn Williams Street and cross the grocery store's parking lot to access Hanna Avenue.

West Elm

You'll pass by a **Starbucks** with decent patio before reaching **West Elm**.

8 The architecture of the building by the entrance (currently hosting **Yogurty's** over two floors) blends perfectly with the industrial metal arches leading to the home decor store.

9 **West Elm**'s stylish showroom is huge, it covers the whole block!

The courtyard by **West Elm** is well landscaped in the summer and it is better admired from the outdoor patio of **Mildred's Temple Kitchen**.

10 I had lunch inside this beautiful restaurant on a weekday (no line-up then). I expected a stuffier ambiance but was instead seduced by the laid-back feeling of it all.

On the menu, the fries were prescribed as "very good for physiological disorders and hangovers".

Look up inside the building attached to **Mildred's Temple Kitchen** to take in the elegant wire face sculptures suspended from the ceiling.

11 Then, pass along the side of **West Elm**. Turn left on Atlantic Ave. and right on Liberty St. until you reach Mowat Ave., where you'll turn right. The old red brick buildings on this street are majestic and overgrown with ivy.

One of them (by the lower grey building) looks straight out of the *Jack and the Beanstalk* storybook.

This is where you'll find a passage leading into the lanes of the old **Toronto Carpet Factory**.

For maximum effect, I suggest you walk around the block to access the first alley you'll meet.

Fraser Avenue

12 The viewpoint you'll get when entering the old manufacturing facilities from this sheltered alley is that of a scene from the 1880's, with the tall chimney and Victorian buildings.

On the right, you'll reach the classic Italian **Caffino Ristorante**. I found the high ceiling and large windows of this secluded restaurant simply charming.

The place generates good reviews for its classic Italian food. (They serve lunch Monday to Friday from 11:30 a.m. to 3:30 p.m.)

13 Back to the lane, walk south into the parking lot and you'll enjoy the surprising sight of the wonderful mural of a giant rug with colourful intricate design.

14 Further, is the funkiest restaurant in **Liberty Village**: **School Bakery Café**, with black chalkboards and numerous clocks (reminder of when the minutes went by too slowly in the classroom?).

They offer original menus and their daily bakery items are good. (The place opens at 8 a.m. Monday to Friday, and at 9:30 a.m. on weekends.)

15 You'll notice an odd-shaped metal bench at the northeast corner of Fraser and Liberty. It's a xylophone which you can actually try out and it's part of the **BENCHmark Program** responsible for the adorned benches around Liberty Street.

Walking back along Liberty, see the cute mural on **The Roastery** on Pardee Ave. This place and unassuming **Liberty Village Market & Café** on Jefferson Ave. both offer a cheaper fare. (I found the back room in the latter surprisingly pretty.)

16 Turn right on Jefferson and walk through the first small lane on your left to see the line-up of mural paintings.

17 **25 Liberty** (at Liberty and Atlantic) has replaced **Liberty Bistro** and revamped the place and the menu. It is in a great heritage building with an inviting patio for drinks.

18 Finally, there's **Balzac's Coffee Roastery** across from the parking lot at Liberty and Hanna. Looking very Parisian with its intricate floor tiling, it includes a tiny patio during the summer.

QUEEN WEST
BOHEMIAN STROLL
21

Unconventional wisdom is fun

People around here have their own way of doing things. Where else will you find half a Cadillac welded to a facade? A self-proclaimed hoarder who turned his obsession into an Ali Baba's cave filled with crystal, retail collectives of fashion designers and jewelers, and a cool little restaurant lost in the residential area? There's much more thrill of the find to be had with all the vintage furniture and clothing stores. Then, you can push your stroll to the waterfront just across the walkway by Roncesvalles Avenue, for a lovely contrast after your bath in this high-density urban fun.

STROLL 21

Full loop:
3.5 km (55 min)

Shorter version:
One of Queen West's main appeals is the cluster of vintage and antique stores in the area. You could have breakfast at **Mitzi's Café** and walk east on Queen and you'd catch most of them along a 1.6 km stroll (25 min).

Game for more?
The intersection of Roncesvalles Avenue and Queen West is included in the **Sunnyside Endless Stroll** (**Stroll 14**, p. 85).

Parking & TTC
• The streetcar **#501** runs along Queen.
• You can find free street parking on Sorauren and adjacent streets.
• Just east of O'Hara Avenue, there's a **Green P** parking lot at the **Dollarama**.

Other TIPS
• Many antique shops only open from Wednesday to Sunday, at around 11 a.m. It is better to do this stroll on these days, when there is more ambiance in the area.

Sorauren Avenue

1 **Mitzi's Café** is a very popular all-day breakfast place which is true eye candy in the middle of residential Sorauren Avenue. We just love the food, the laid-back ambiance and the location of this place.

If you're starting your stroll later in the day, try instead **Poor John's Café** with great sandwiches and a hidden backyard patio (1610 Queen West, just west of Sorauren).

2 Once you're ready, turn right to start your tour of the antique and vintage stores on this side of Queen West. First, there's **Frou Frou Vintage** (1616 Queen West). Further west, check the window of the venue/workshop **Sixth Gallery** (1642); it usually features funky little robots.

Past Triller Street is a cluster of great vintage stores to explore: **Mostly Movables**, **Arcadia Antiques**, **1968 Queen Antiques**, to name a few.

3 We thought there was some truly artistic displays going on at **Black Pug** (1712).

4 Next door, **Soda Bar** is totally different, more whimsical with vivid retro items. It is followed by more serious **James Dys Antiques & Collectibles** filled with classy finds.

Beaty Parkette

5 Did you know you can access the beach by taking the pedestrian bridge to the right of **Beaty Parkette** (at the foot of Roncesvalles and Queen)?

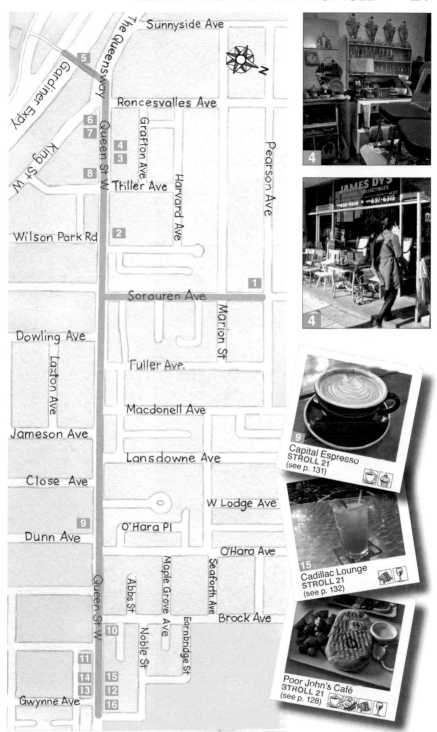

Capital Espresso
STROLL 21
(see p. 131)

Cadillac Lounge
STROLL 21
(see p. 132)

Poor John's Café
STROLL 21
(see p. 128)

It is worth taking 5 minutes to cross over, just to admire the view.

Queen Street West

6 **Easy Restaurant,** on the south side of the road at 1645 Queen West is an easy-going all-day breakfast, lunch and dinner place. It is bigger than it looks, with an additional section in the back. (You've got to check out the retro billboard they put up along King West!)

7 **Sam The Chandelier Man** (1663) has been a fixture forever in Parkdale (no pun intended!). If you're the kind of woman to be distracted by all things shiny, you'll never get out of this filled-to-the-brim chandelier store.

Nearby **Stella Luna** usually has a very good collection of vintage clothes.

8 Further east, **Hideway Antiques** (1605) includes large scale items (15-foot wide billboard anyone?) and surprising items amidst a wide selection of vintage wooden furniture.

Some creepy (but utterly cool) antique mechanical clowns were staring at us when we visited.

The Queen West Antique Centre next door is a vast store with very eclectic vintage items organized in what looks like an already livable fashion. (Making it easier to imagine what it would look like in one's home.)

After that, there are a few bland blocks to stroll through before it gets interesting again. (I noticed a few Tibetan shops and restaurants.)

9 Further east, there's vintage clothing shop **Common Sort** (1414 Queen West) and, across the street, the alluring **Capital Espresso**, serving scrumptious muffins with their excellent coffee. (I think this is where I've had the smoothest latte in town!)

The big **Dollarama**'s parking lot (past Dunn Avenue) is a good place to park if you want to start your stroll with a visit to fantastic **Designer Fabrics** (1360 Queen West) selling all kinds of fabric over two floors.

This destination is a must if you're shopping for fabric. They rent large samples to help you visualize how it would look with the rest of your home decor.

Brock Avenue

East of Brock is another cluster of great shops (this time with a focus on fashion, contemporary and vintage). Brace yourself for some serious window shopping.

10 The boutique **Shopgirls** (at 1342 Queen West) is a design collective featuring the creations of Canadian artists and designers. They're also the Yoga Jeans experts (having fitted over 5,000 women with them) and offer free hemming on regular priced jeans!

It is followed by **The Workroom** (where anyone can pay by the hour to use their equipment to sew their own projects).

Next door is also busy with artists at work. **Made You Look** (1338) showcases the work of over 100 Toronto jewelry designers.

11 The **Mascot** is a cool café/gallery with interesting art (267 Queen West).

12 **The Public Butter** (1290), an off-shoot of **Black Market Vintage Clothing**, is packed with casual vintage clothes and T-shirts.

13 Facing it on the south side of Queen, **House of Vintage** offers fancier clothes. (I saw many dreamy dresses from the 50s and wonderful leather items.)

14 Along the way, there are a few original options if you'd like to stop for a drink during the day. The **Stones Place** (filled with Rolling Stones paraphernalia) only opens after 8 p.m. but **The Rhino**'s large patio next door (1249) is quite appealing on a bright sunny day. (You go there for the ambiance when it's busy and for some beer, but don't expect cocktails.)

15 Some say that the **Cadillac Lounge** across the street (1296) will bring out the Thelma and Louise in you. This rockabilly place features a line-up of great bands in the evenings and late afternoon on weekends. (They open at 11 a.m. on weekdays and 10:30 on weekends and serve food.)

Walk through the dark retro pub and you'll reach a surprisingly large backyard patio, open year-round. We had a sparkling Pink Cadillac.

16 Food wise, I've had a very good and well priced grilled cheese at cosy **Rustic Cosmo Cafe** (1278). They open at 9 a.m. on weekdays, Saturdays at 9:30 a.m., Sundays at 10 a.m.

Sun and the City

Nowhere else in Toronto will you get this vantage point of a sunset over the city. Broadview overlooks **River-dale Park East**, with downtown's high-rises in the background. Lately, things got even better, thanks to the **Rooster Coffee House**. In the fall, when the sun sets before their closing time, they supply blankets for those who want to sit outside and enjoy the view. To kill time while you wait for your sunset, you can access a walkway crossing over the Don Valley Parkway to reach Cabbagetown. Or you could have a bite at nearby **Hanoi 3 Seasons**, a local Vietnamese restaurant and admire the **Toronto Chinese Archway** on the way.

STROLL 22

Full loop:
4.8 km (1 hr 15 min)

Shorter version:
A shorter 1.8 km stroll (30 min) along **Riverdale Park East** and over the Don Valley Parkway will allow you to fully enjoy the view.

Game for more?
Riverdale Park West, across from the pedestrian bridge, touches the **Cabbagetown Nooks & Crannies Stroll** (**Stroll 15**, p. 91).

Parking & TTC
• Exit at **Broadview Subway Station**.
• I usually park on Langley Ave., east of Broadview. It's allowed after 10 a.m.
• After 9 a.m., you might find room on Broadview along the park.

Other TIPS
• On **www.timeanddate.com** (click *Sun & Moon*) I found the following sunset times for Toronto:
May 1st (8:20 p.m.), June 1st (8:50 p.m.), July 1st (9 p.m.), August 1st (8:40 p.m.), September 1st (7:50 p.m.), and October 1st (7 p.m.).

Riverdale Park East

1 I like to park on Langley Avenue, near **Rooster Coffee House**.

The goal for this stroll is to fully enjoy the sunset over Toronto's cityscape. And to succeed, there are two things to consider: the current sunset time, and the fact that **Rooster Coffee House** is open 7 a.m. to 7 p.m., year-round.

My favourite scenario is in October, when the sun sets at 7 p.m. or earlier, pretty much in front of the café. You'll be able to sit at their outdoor patio with a blanket on your knees (courtesy of the café), to observe the sun disappear behind the urban horizon, while sipping a hot coffee.

2 At any other time of the year, make sure you're anywhere along **Riverdale Park East** by Broadview Avenue 15 minutes prior to the sunset time.

You'll find some benches along Broadview but many like to sit on the grassy slope to watch the "show" (on a blanket).

Note that in the summer, the sun sets more to the northern side of the park.

Riverdale Park West

3 If you arrive awhile before the sunset, you'll have time to walk down the steep slope of the park to reach the pedestrian bridge running over the Don Valley Pkwy.

It gives a great view over **Riverdale Park East**, on one side, and **Riverdale Park West** on the other side of the highway.

Broadview
Station

Danforth Ave

9

Dearbourne Ave

Fairview Blvd

Broadview Ave

10

Hogarth Ave

Montcrest
Blvd

Riverdale
Pool

Don Valley Pkwy

Bayview Ave

2 Bain Ave

Broadview Ave

Riverdale
Park

3

4

1
11

5

6 Langley Ave

Victor Ave

9
Allen's
STROLL 22
(see p. 137)

8
Hanoi 3 Seasons
STROLL 22
(see p. 136)

11
Rooster Coffee House
STROLL 22
(see p. 137)

Gerrard St E

7

8

N

135

4 Follow the paved path on the other side of the bridge and you'll get to the staircase leading to Carlton Street and **Riverdale Farm**.

5 The panorama from Riverdale Park Road along the upper part of **Riverdale Park West** is worth the climb. (From the **Rooster** to this point and back, it is a 1.75 km stroll (30 min).

Broadview Avenue

6 Back to Broadview Avenue, following the gravel path to the right of the park, you'll see a heritage wooden clubhouse with a long porch, which was transported here from its initial location on Gerrard Street.

7 Take your right on Broadview Avenue, then cross Gerrard Street and turn right to reach the impressive traditional Chinese **Zhong Hua Men Archway**... in a 40-space parking lot.

It is easier to appreciate the intricate details of the carving in the bas-relief all around the structure when they are lit at night (which makes this a good stroll to do after you've watched your sunset).

8 If you still have one hour to go before the sunset and you feel hungry, I recommend the Vietnamese cuisine of the small restaurant **Hanoi 3 Seasons** (588 Gerrard Street East), in the small Chinatown. It is open daily from 11 a.m. to 10 p.m.

It will take you 5 minutes to walk from that restaurant back to the park.

Danforth Avenue

9 When it's patio season, I recommend you take advantage of this stroll to have a drink or a bite in the backyard patio of **Allen's** (143 Danforth Avenue). The food is fancier and a bit more expensive than one would assume in a pub but their terrace is unique. The daylight is gorgeous when filtered by the gigantic willow trees towering over the patio and at night, lights give them a dramatic effect.

10 It takes approximately 15 minutes to walk from **Allen's** back to the park. Along the way, there are some majestic houses to admire on the west side of Broadview, before you reach the park.

Rooster Coffee House

11 The stroll around **Riverdale Park East** and over the Don Valley Pkwy is enjoyable even if you can't make it work around the sunset. And we have **Rooster Coffee House** (479 Broadview Avenue) to thank for that. Ever since they opened, they've injected life (and serious caffeine) into the area.

The place is welcoming, with a communal table in the back and plenty of books and games for the customers. There are pastries under glass bell jars, little trinkets to look at amidst the treats, great coffee, binoculars by the window, and cool people behind the counter. (In the winter, they dress up the rooster on their sign.)

A very yummy stroll

This little stretch of Queen East is growing fast. I can't keep track of the new businesses opening and I live in the area. **Dark Horse Espresso Bar** and **Merchants of Green Coffee** are reasons enough to visit this part of town. But so are **Bonjour Brioche**'s flaky croissants, the **Ambiance**'s delicious (and affordable) chocolates, the **Mary Macleod's Shortbread** gourmet cookies, the scones, the pies, the cupcakes, the olives... And then, there are the restaurants. Isn't it convenient that the **Don Trail** running along the river is just down the bridge to help us burn off those calories?

STROLL 23

Full loop:
1.8 km (30 min)

Shorter version:
If you stick to the Queen Street East stretch in Riverside, it is a .8 km loop which takes less than 15 minutes to stroll back and forth.

Game for more?
The **Leslieville Hipster Stroll** (**Stroll 19**, p. 115) starts where **Stroll 23** stops, east of **Jimmie Simpson Park**. If you follow the trail going south, down the stairs by the Queen East bridge, it will lead you to **The Distillery Red Brick Stroll** (**Stroll 7**, p. 43) in 1.6 km (20 min).

Parking & TTC
• The streetcar **#501** runs along Queen.
• You can easily find street parking after 10 a.m. on the streets north and south of Queen Street East.

Other TIPS
• I prefer not to do this stroll on Mondays, when many shops are closed. Many restaurants tend to be closed at lunch time when summer is over.

Matilda Street

1 Merchants of Green Coffee (2 Matilda St.) is one of the best kept secrets in the area. I like to park on quaint little Hamilton St. (arriving from Dundas, west of Broadview Ave.). Then I walk south and turn right on Kintyre Ave. (it becomes Matilda St.).

The café is at the turn in the road, hidden beneath a green canopy in the summer (open weekdays 8 a.m. to 6 p.m., weekends 10 a.m. to 6 p.m.).

It is as cool as can be (you can bring your own food since they just carry a few treats), with a cosy cottage feeling, thanks to all the wood, the roaming cat, the old piano and shelves loaded with books.

Next, I suggest you stroll the neighbourhood by going east on Matilda. **Joel Weeks Park** on your right is a lovely addition to the neighbourhood.

2 Cross Broadview Avenue and you'll see the artisanal **St. John's Bakery**. **3** Keep walking on Kintyre Avenue and turn right on Grant Street (one of the prettiest streets in the area). Then take your left on Clark Street, and turn right on Boulton Avenue. Lovely, isn't it?

Excellent **Bonjour Brioche Bakery Café** is right at the corner of Boulton and Queen (open at 8 a.m., closed on Mondays). It's very popular.

If it is full when you show up for breakfast or lunch, there's a second best option nearby: **The Canadian Pie Company** at 798 Queen East.

Queen Street East

4 For a quick look at an inspiring project, go left under the viaduct adorned with murals, and check the little **McClearen Playground** to your right. Almost everything in there was created out of a huge mature tree from that park which had to be cut down.

5 Around **Bonjour Brioche**, you'll find vintage clothing at **Common Sort**, some funky clothes and shoes at **Bergstrom**, and **Olive and Olives**, a beautiful specialty store.

Phil'z (792 Queen E., across the street) carries truly original furniture and spectacular lamps.

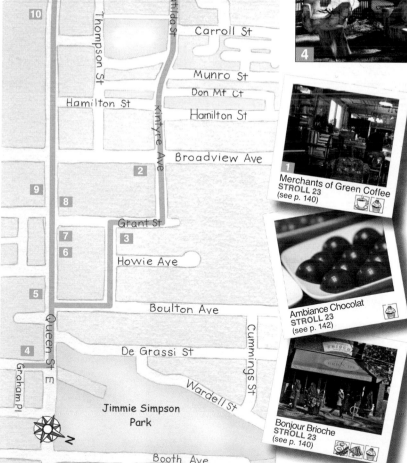

Merchants of Green Coffee
STROLL 23
(see p. 140)

Ambiance Chocolat
STROLL 23
(see p. 142)

Bonjour Brioche
STROLL 23
(see p. 140)

6 A bit further west, is **Hardware Interiors**, another great furniture shop at 760 Queen East.

7 Beyond, you'll see the beautiful building hosting the fancy clothes of **Stephan Caras**, sided by **Desmond & Beatrice** cup cakes, and facing excellent **Ambiance Chocolat** (753-A).

8 Gastronomical **Ruby Watch** (offering only one table d'hôte option per night) owns **Ruby Eats**. The gorgeous food shop down the block at 742 now serves lunch at small tables.

9 They face the vintage store **Studio Pazo**.

Empire by bullet sits across the street from **Pulp Kitchen** (the tiniest take-out shop, with an orange facade at 717 1/2).

Beyond that, there's more to discover: the messages engraved in the sidewalks at the Broadview intersection, the architectural details of **Jilly's** (a strip club...), the great **Dark Horse Espresso Bar** with communal table (682 Queen East).

10 There's a surprising backyard patio at **F' Coffee** (serving beer) by **Mary Macleod's Shortbread** at 639 Queen East.

11 You can then cross the bridge for a great view over the Don River.

If you go down the stairs on the west side of the bridge (south side of Queen), you will reach the **Don Trail** running along the river.

Once you're done, go north on Davis Avenue to return to Matilda Street.

ROSEDALE
MEANDERING STROLL
24

The "crème de la crème" of strolls

There's more to this delightful stroll amidst one of Toronto's wealthiest neighbourhoods than meets the eye. It includes the prettiest access to **Evergreen Brick Works** via ravine trails, **Chorley Park** (one of Toronto's best parks), a few raised walkways offering a lovely view over surprising streets with a true countryside feel. On the only commercial stretch in this residential area, you'll find a convenience store selling **Balzac's** coffee (to start you on the right foot) and the fabulous **Summerhill Market** with fine grocery and take-out of all kinds (for a big finish before heading home).

Full loop:
5.8 km (1 hr 30 min)

Shorter version:
The first part of the stroll up Rosedale Heights Dr. and back is the most beautiful "country road" in the city, ending at Mount Pleasant (a return 2-km stroll, 30 min).

Game for more?
Chorley Park, which is just at the end of Summerhill Avenue, is included in the **Don Valley Evergreen Brick Works Stroll** (**Stroll 12**, p. 73).

Parking & TTC
• Bus **#82** runs from **Rosedale Station** to Summerhill Avenue.
• It's easy to find free street parking after 10 a.m. north of Summerhill Avenue.
• You can park on Hudson Dr. and start the stroll at the Heath St. pedestrian bridge.

Other TIPS
• **Summerhill Market** offers delicious prepared food you might want to bring back home so you don't have to cook tonight (great pasta deals).

Summerhill Avenue

1 There are a couple of things I did not expect to find in posh Rosedale: the quaint country feeling of Summerhill Avenue up MacLennan Avenue, and the trendy **Summerhill Market** in the middle of this residential area.

I found free parking on the streets near the market and came back to explore the upscale grocery store. Wow! What a spread! (You've got to check their website at www.summerhill-market.com to get an idea.) It was lunch time when we visited so my girlfriend and I each got a tasty sandwich to go.

As we walked west, we found out that **Scoops**, the local convenience store at 428 Summerhill Avenue (also managed by **Summerhill Market**), serves **Balzac's** coffee, the same brand as the one found at **The Distillery**.

2 Keep walking west and you'll be able to climb a ramp to cross over the train tracks. (Make sure you look east over the tracks to catch a genuine country sight.)

MacLennan Avenue

3 On the other side of the tracks, walk down the stairs and around the corner to your right to stroll part of bucolic Carstowe Road.

4 Then, go up MacLennan Avenue (noticeable for the mural on the right wall). Keep going north to Inglewood Drive, where you turn right, then left onto Welland Avenue.

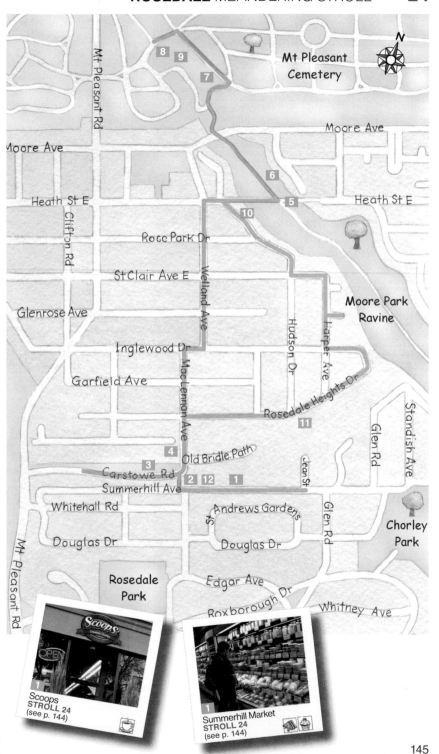

8 9

7

Mt Pleasant
Cemetery

N

Moore Ave

Moore Ave

6

Heath St E

5

Heath St E

10

Rose Park Dr

St Clair Ave E

Welland Ave

Glenrose Ave

Moore Park
Ravine

Inglewood Dr

Hudson Dr

Harper Ave

Rosedale Heights Dr

11

Garfield Ave

MacLennan Ave

Standish Ave

4

Old Bridle Path

Glen Rd

3

Carstowe Rd

2 12   1

Summerhill Ave

Jean St

Whitehall Rd

St Andrews Gardens

Glen Rd

Chorley
Park

Douglas Dr

Douglas Dr

Clifton Rd

Mt Pleasant Rd

Rosedale
Park

Edgar Ave

Roxborough Dr

Whitney Ave

Mt Pleasant Rd

1
Scoops
STROLL 24
(see p. 144)

1
Summerhill Market
STROLL 24
(see p. 144)

Heath Street East

5 On Heath Street East, turn right to reach the pedestrian bridge passing over the **Moore Park Ravine** trail and **Mud Creek**. The passage is lovely in the summer but truly spectacular when all the leaves are in full colour.

Turn left again after the bridge to reach the trail, where you'll turn right. (Note that if you turned left on the trail, you would reach **Don Valley Brick Works** in about 15 minutes.)

Moore Park Ravine

6 Along the way, when you have a chance, have a look at the river running down the ravine.

The trees provide a most welcome shade in the heat of the summer. You'll notice a pond to your right before the trail goes up to Moore Avenue.

Across the street, you'll reach **Mount Pleasant Cemetery**. The Moore entrance is no longer accessible by car since they added the new Visitation Centre in 2009. But a bike trail runs through this entrance.

Into the cemetery

7 Follow the blue line on the ground. It will lead you to the **Forest of Remembrance**, where mature trees tower over natural rocks bearing memorial plates.

It will take you to the iron gate of Section 22, beyond which await two graceful geese in flight and the romantic sculpture of an embracing couple.

8 Further, you'll reach the beautiful **Garden of Remembrance** with its **Pool of Reflection** and **River of Memories**, providing all kinds of memorial options for those who chose cremation.

The attention to detail is quite impressive all around, down to the bike racks! (They look like pieces of art and a sign explains they are the winning design of a Bicycle Rack Design Competition held in 2010 by **Ryerson University** with **Mount Pleasant Cemetery**.)

9 When we visited in July, we noticed the ground was peppered with colourful pinwheels on our way back to the forest. It turns out they were decorating a whole section of plaques for infants...

Hudson Drive

10 Walk back to the trail across Moore Avenue and the Heath Street pedestrian bridge. Then turn left on Hudson Drive, for a taste of the Rosedale neighbourhood.

Keep to your left to St. Clair Avenue East, it becomes Harper Avenue. (Check the lovely dead-end of Valley View to your left.)

11 Then turn left again on Inglewood Drive. It becomes Rosedale Heights Drive, which you'll follow until you reach MacLennan Avenue.

12 Then it's back over the pedestrian bridge to Summerhill Avenue (to your car and your take-out dinner from **Summerhill Market**).

THE BEACH
QUAINT STROLL
25

With a beach down the street

To fully enjoy the quaint neighbourhood of **The Beach**, drive past the busiest part of Queen East (around **Kew Gardens**) and park anywhere east of the lovely ravine by Glen Manor Drive. Peek southbound down any of the streets from there to Victoria Park Avenue and you're sure to see a picture-perfect little dead-end road framed by gorgeous cottages and running into a patch of the sparkling lake topped with an arch of tall trees. Explore the streets north of Queen to admire more beautiful houses perched on top of steep hills. On Queen, you'll find the best salty muffins, chocolates, pies...

STROLL 25

Full loop:
6.6 km (1 hr 40 min)

Shorter version:
The following circuit is 2.5 km long (40 min). From the mural at the southwest corner of Wineva Avenue and Queen, go to Silverbirch Avenue (past the **Fox Theatre**), then walk down to the beach. Continue on the boardwalk to your right, up to Hammersmith Avenue (where houses sit by the boardwalk), and back to Queen.

Game for more?
Enter **Ivan Forrest Gardens** and continue into **Glen Stewart Park** to reach the ravine across the street (a 2 km return walk).

Parking & TTC
• The streetcar **#501** runs along Queen E.
• The farther east of **Kew Gardens**, the easier to find free street parking north and south of Queen.

Other TIPS
• Go to **www.fox-theatre.ca** for their movie listing (2236 Queen E.).

East end

1 The farther you are from **Kew Gardens**, the easier it is to find street parking. I prefer parking on the streets east of Glen Manor Drive around Beech Avenue, because it is close to my darling coffee shop in the area, **Remarkable Bean** at 2242 Queen East. (Try their decadent salty muffins!)

This section is really charming, with adjacent **Luberon** filled with French merchandise, **Mira's** consignment store, **Fox Theatre** and **Ed's Real Scoop**'s gelato made from scratch, further west.

2 Facing **Ed's** is **Chocolate by Wickerhead Co.** (2375 Queen East) with exquisite artisanal chocolates at a good price, and the family restaurant **Garden Gate**.

3 Walk east on Queen Street for a little immersion in **The Beach** neighbourhood. You can see the lake glistening at the end of every street south of Queen.

4 Check Neville Park Boulevard north of Queen for some great properties perched on top of steep front yards. Return on Queen and turn right, passing by **Life is Sweet** bakery (2328 Queen East).

5 Then turn left at Munro Park to reach the secluded part of **Balmy Beach** with dreamy houses.

You can take Willow Avenue (by **Balmy Beach Club**), turn left on Park Avenue, and right on Beech, to get back to Queen, where you'll turn left.

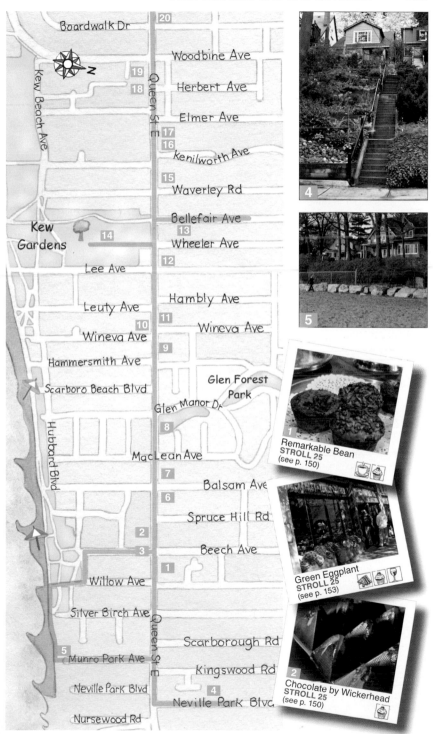

Boardwalk Dr

20

N

Woodbine Ave

19

18

Herbert Ave

Elmer Ave

Kenilworth Ave

17

16

Kew Beach Ave

Queen St E

15

Waverley Rd

Bellefair Ave

13

Kew
Gardens

14

Wheeler Ave

12

Lee Ave

Leuty Ave

Hambly Ave

11

10

Wineva Ave

Wineva Ave

9

Hammersmith Ave

Glen Forest
Park

Scarboro Beach Blvd

Glen Manor Dr

8

Hubbard Blvd

MacLean Ave

7

Balsam Ave

6

Spruce Hill Rd

2

3

Beech Ave

1

Willow Ave

Silver Birch Ave

Queen St E

5

Scarborough Rd

Munro Park Ave

Kingswood Rd

Neville Park Blvd

4

Neville Park Blvd

Nursewood Rd

4

5

1
Remarkable Bean
STROLL 25
(see p. 150)

Green Eggplant
STROLL 25
(see p. 153)

2
Chocolate by Wickerhead
STROLL 25
(see p. 150)

Some points of interest along your way to **Ivan Forrest Gardens**:

6 **Arts-on-Queen** artists store (2198 Queen E.).

7 Lovely **Tori's Bakeshop** (2188), next to unique **Curvaceous Consignments** (2186), a resale boutique for sizes 14+.

Glen Manor Drive

8 Then, you arrive at **Ivan Forrest Gardens** by Glen Manor Drive. This little park is beautiful and leads to **Glen Forest Park** and its ravine.

It faces **The Pie Shack** at 2305 Queen (very cool with a large pie hanging from the upper window). This place serves huge pieces of pie. It has a lovely French country feeling to it and its cupboards are filled with games and books for their customers.

Some of the shops I like to visit between there and **Kew Gardens** are: **Aix-En-Tric** jewelry boutique (2144), **Mastermind Toys**, clothing store **Set Me Free**, gadget shop **Stack** and **Modern Tibet** (for the exotic jewelry).

9 I can't wait to try **Castro's Lounge** (2116), serving vegetarian food and serious beer and featuring live music.

10 There's a great mural at the southeast corner of Queen and Wineva. We've had original breakfast crepes at **Juice and Java** at 2102 Queen E.

11 **Pippins Tea Company** (2096) has to be the quaintest shop on the street!

Kids at Home (2086 Queen East) and **Nesters**, across the street, are both fun to explore.

12 Across from **Coles** bookstore (2169), there's another ambitious mural on the **Beach Foodland**.

Then, facing **Kew Gardens**, are **Mendecino** (bargain outlet), **Posh** (filled with beautiful clothes for all occasions) and **Walking on a Cloud**, a big shoe store with a wide selection.

Bellefair Avenue

13 Stroll a few blocks north of Queen, along Bellefair Avenue to see more of the residential area. I think the combination of road inclination, tall trees and high ratio of wooden houses on that street, contribute to the charming impression.

14 Across from Bellefair is **Kew Gardens**. I recommend you walk down the path on the west side of the public library to admire the gardens, the gazebo amidst the trees, and the park keeper's beautiful heritage house.

West of Bellefair Avenue, is my favourite **Starbucks** in the city. It has a fireplace, cosy sofas and an outdoor patio.

Further west, **The Embellishment Room** (1978) offers plenty of interesting clothes $30 a piece.

15 It is followed by **The Artisans**, **Seagull Classics** and **Potala Gifts**, three good shops to sift through.

We've enjoyed many meals in the colourful **Green Eggplant** (1968).

16 Other interesting options for their patios, weather permitting, are **Lion on the Beach** (1958 Queen East) and the neat backyard patio (which you can't see from the street) of **Beach Bird**, across the street.

17 Beyond **Book City** (1950), you'll find **Corso Shoes** (1942), **Binz**, all about storage solutions (1934) and **Ends** (1930) where you can usually find amazing bargains on the sidewalk or inside.

18 Past Elmer Street, are a few more interesting boutiques: **Mourguet** (with great jewelry) and **Moo Milk Bar** (with the best cookies!).

They are facing **Ella Minnow Children's Bookstore** (1915) and **Dufflet** next door. (Have a look at the slick eating area in the back of this bakery. It offers a wonderful oasis!)

Woodbine Avenue

19 In the funky gallery-café **Wunderland** (located in front of the fire hall with heritage tower), I noticed that the barista bore an airy resemblance to the man portrayed on the naive paintings!

20 Just west of Woodbine Avenue is **The Wardrobe Designer** (1878 1/2), a unique boutique offering creations including pieces of vintage fabric in their designs.

Finally, one block further, there's the great French **Zane Patisserie** (1842), with a few tables. Time to refill before heading east towards your starting point. Bon appétit!

TRINITY-BELLWOODS
ARTSY STROLL
26

Creative take on life

The **Museum of Contemporary Canadian Art** near **Trinity-Bellwoods Park** sets the artsy tone of this stroll. Even if you don't enter into this pay-what-you-can cutting edge museum, there's always some major outdoor artwork to be admired from the sidewalk. Local bakery **Nadège Patisserie** sells seriously artistic edible creations. Between the park and Bathurst, you'll find over 30 original fashion stores (I counted them!). West of the park, knitting gets über cool with **Knit Café**'s funky window. Galleries abound, and at **Gladstone Hotel**, one-of a-kind guest rooms open into a lobby-gallery on every floor. Art is everywhere!

STROLL
26

Full loop:
4.8 km (1 hr 15 min)

Shorter version:
The fashion loop (including **Trinity-Bellwoods Park** and Queen W., east of the park), is 2.6 km long (40 min). The artsy loop west of **Trinity-Bellwoods Park**, including a stroll in the park, is 3 km long (45 min).

Game for more?
The **Queen West Bohemian Stroll** (**Stroll 21**, p. 127) is just west of this stroll and **Queen Street Smart Stroll** (**Stroll 4**, p. 29) just east of it.

Parking & TTC
• The streetcar **#501** runs along Queen.
• There's a **Green P** lot at 803 Richmond St., south of Queen. Lisgar St. and Beaconsfield Ave., north of Queen, are good for free parking.

Other TIPS
• Many stores are closed on Mondays.
• **Trinity-Bellwoods Farmers' Market** is open on Tuesdays, 3 p.m. to 7 p.m., from May to October.

Dundas West
I like to start this stroll with a walk through **Trinity-Bellwoods Park**. (Beatrice Street and Montrose Avenue, north of the park, offer free parking after 7 a.m.)

Almost facing the park, you'll find **The Tampered Press** espresso bar at Crawford and Dundas West.

1 We can't see it from the street, but there's a huge natural pit in the northern part of the park. Standing at the bottom of the bowl, we can see the **CN Tower** pop out of the horizon on the east side.

2 A path bordered with mature trees leads to the majestic black iron gates of the park's entrance on Queen West.

East of the park
I suggest you begin with the fashion loop to your left on Queen while you're still fresh. In the five blocks between Bellwoods and Bathurst, I've counted over 30 fashion boutiques selling original merchandise you don't usually find anywhere else.

3 Since this is the Artsy Stroll, it is appropriate to mention that there are two showroom/studios you could visit in the area if the artists are available. There's very approachable designer Yasmine Louis on Niagara (see **www.yasminelouis.com**), whose silk-screened T-shirts bear quotes such as "*I lied and went to see a matinee*". And the whimsical fabric designer behind **www.peachbeserck.com** (with a new studio on Shaw Street).

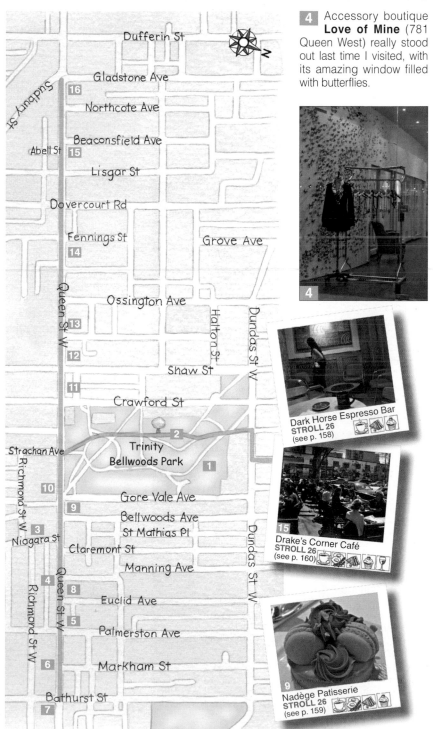

4 Accessory boutique **Love of Mine** (781 Queen West) really stood out last time I visited, with its amazing window filled with butterflies.

Dark Horse Espresso Bar
STROLL 26
(see p. 158)

Drake's Corner Café
STROLL 26
(see p. 160)

Nadège Patisserie
STROLL 26
(see p. 159)

5 **Fresh Collective** (692 Queen West) showcase the original creations of small designers while **Cabaret** (672) is a one-of-a-kind high-end vintage clothes store.

Between the park and just east of Bathurst, you can also expect about fifteen furniture and home decor stores.

6 Among my favourites: **Chatelet** with its shabby-chic French flair (699), **Neat**'s assortment of storage solutions (628) and **Morba**'s wonderful bric-a-brac collection (665).

7 I loved the layout (and the artwork) inside the huge furniture store **Design Republic** sitting at 639, east of Bathurst.

Remix Clothing (next door on the 2nd floor) is a luxury resale store carrying serious names: Louboutin, Prada and the likes. (So does **Fashionably Yours** at 632.)

For some edgy design, have a look at **Dark Horse Espresso Bar** (684).

There's also the funky rooftop patio (with heaters to stretch the season) of **Czehoski** (678).

I can really picture my girlfriends and I on that rooftop with a $15 artisanal cheese board and some wine! (I've seen the place open earlier than 3 p.m. when the weather gets warmer. Check their website for their current hours.)

8 **Red Tea Box**'s pastries look spectacular (696). Their tea selection is quite impressive and served in delicate china. They offer a lunch menu and a high tea as well.

Their main room is charming, and I felt like a child entering her first tree house when I passed through the narrow courtyard to access their unique secluded back room.

By the park

9 There's no secret room in Zen **Nadège Patisserie** (780 Queen West) but their pastries are delectable pieces of culinary art. (Their outdoor patio is nicely adorned with flowers and facing the park.)

10 Directly across the street from **Trinity-Bellwoods Park**, you'll find **Preloved** (a fantastic store filled with ingenious designs which have turned boring clothes into funky apparel), **Type Books** (offering an original book selection) and **The Paper Place** (featuring the most exciting assortment of papers).

I'm a big fan of nearby **Chippy's** golden thick fries (893).

West of the park

There are about 20 art galleries between **Trinity-Bellwoods Park** and the **Gladstone Hotel**.

11 I encourage you to peek through the fence into the the private gardens of **Artscape** on your way (900) and to check the top of the building.

12 **MOCCA** is the must destination at 952 (a pay-what-you-can museum). You never know what public art to expect in the vast outdoor space they share with **Edward Day Gallery**.

13 More great places between **MOCCA** and the **Drake Hotel** are all yours to discover such as **BYOB** at 972 Queen W. (vintage absinthe fountain, anyone?). Make sure to check out **Knit Café**'s window (1050). Knitting doesn't get cooler than this; once, it featured a knitted blazing fire with roasting marshmallows.

14 I also love **69 Vintage Store** (1100).

Beaconsfield Avenue

Mabel's opened its second bakery at 1156, west of Beaconsfield Avenue.

On the south side of Queen, at Beaconsfield, you'll find **Woolfitt's Art Supplies** (now part of Curry's).

15 On the north side is the famous **Drake Hotel** (1150), preceded by the **Drake General Store**, filled with trinkets.

Drake's Corner Café opens daily at 7:30 a.m. and spreads into the outdoor patio. Their splendid **Sky Yard** rooftop opens in the evening. (Have a peek at the hip decor in their dinning room!)

16 A few blocks further west, and you've arrived at the **Gladstone Hotel** (1214). Their café opens daily at 7 a.m.

This hotel features 37 artist-designed rooms. Consult their scrapbook at the reception, or visit **www.gladstonehotel.com**, to see all the designs.

You'll find a lobby gallery at every floor, which you can visit during daytime. They will gladly take you to the upper floors on their vintage brass elevator.

The life of an urban cottager

As you walk along the carless streets of the most intriguing neighbourhood of Toronto, you'll start to wonder what it would feel like to leave the big city behind after a day's work and return to the cocoon of your cottage-like home on **Toronto Islands**. Most visitors stick to **Ward's** but there are more residences to be seen on adjacent **Algonquin Island**. The secluded boardwalk on the south shore overlooks the expanse of glistening water. Enjoy a glass of wine on the patio of nearby **Rectory Café** and your experience of an urban cottager's lifestyle is complete.

STROLL
27

Full loop:
5.5 km (1 hr 25 min)

Shorter version:
Just do the 2 km **Ward's** loop (30 min).

Game for more?
If you keep walking for 15 minutes further west, past **Snake Island**, you'll reach the belvedere of **Gibraltar Beach**, overlooking the lake. Then, you can walk back to **Ward's Island** along the boardwalk. It will get you to the ferry dock in about 30 minutes.

Parking & TTC
• **Union Subway Station** is a 10-min. walk from the ferry.
• The parking lot at Queens Quay and Lower Simcoe has decent prices (also a 10-min. walk).

Other TIPS
• Carefully note the **Ward's Ferry**'s schedule. It could be one hour between ferries.
• I've visited **Ward's Island** in December under a snow flurry and it was lovely. (**Rectory Café** closes Mondays and Tuesdays in the winter.)

Ward's Island

1 This stroll starts with a ferry ride at the foot of Bay Street. (Make sure you catch the **Ward's Ferry**.)

2 Dozens of bikes greeted us on the deck when we last visited. To your left, you can see a small beach. (In the summer, when you wait for the ferry just before the sunset, it is the perfect spot to catch the sky taking on dreamy pastel hues.)

3 Walk left on Channel Avenue, then start your tour of **Ward's** residential section turning left on 5th Street, walking straight to 3rd Street. Turn left again on Channel and right on 1st Street (peeking through every lane along the way).

4 It is funny to see signs for streets and avenues in this carless environment.

Walk east on Lakeshore Avenue, with one last turn right into 4th Street and around to 5th Street before heading towards the beach.

5 The boardwalk starts by **Ward's Beach**.

6 A couple of minutes further west, you'll find the **Rectory Café** (where I love to end the stroll on their patio with a glass of wine).

7 Walking along the boardwalk, with an endless horizon to your left, is so soothing.

If you continue to the end of the boardwalk and back, it will add 30 minutes to your stroll. (Make sure you have time to catch your ferry ride.)

Instead, I suggest you backtrack and take the lane just west of **Rectory Café** to get to **Snake Island**.

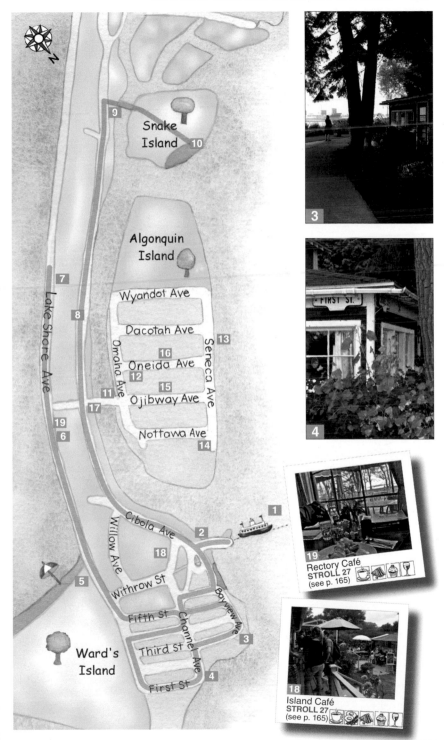

Snake Island

Algonquin Island

Wyandot Ave

Dacotah Ave

Oneida Ave

Ojibway Ave

Nottawa Ave

Omaha Ave

Seneca Ave

Lake Shore Ave

Cibola Ave

Willow Ave

Withrow St

Fifth St

Third St

First St

Channel Ave

Bayview Ave

Ward's Island

FIRST ST.

Rectory Café
STROLL 27
(see p. 165)

Island Café
STROLL 27
(see p. 165)

8 Walk north along that lane and turn left on Cibola Avenue. You'll pass **Algonquin Island** (with a few cool boathouses). Then, you'll reach the bridge to **Snake Island**.

Snake Island

9 From the bridge, you can see a secluded beach by the canal (which gets smelly in the summer!). Straight ahead is a trail leading to the other side of the Island, facing Toronto.

10 When visiting, we saw some fun rogue art by the water (a funky tree stump).

Algonquin Island

11 Walking back to Cibola, turn left, then cross over the pedestrian bridge to **Algonquin Island**. (By the bridge, we noticed a trading cart where it appears the residents drop off what they don't use and take what they need.)

It is quite entertaining to notice all the little details revealing what it must be like to live here. We saw people on bikes carrying huge balls. (They were heading to their gym class in the local community centre on Wyandot Avenue.)

12 Turn left on Omaha Avenue (you'll walk past a great tree house), then turn right on Dacotah Avenue, where you'll see the **CN Tower** pointing at the end of the street.

On that lane, we saw an intriguing giant hand covered in mosaic.

13 Turning right on Seneca Avenue, you get a full view of Toronto's cityscape.

13 Go right on Nottawa Avenue (after having a good look at the house down Seneca, by the yacht club).

14 Back to Omaha Avenue, turn right at the huge cluster of tree stumps. Walk up Ojibway Avenue, lined with pine trees and where a very old tree is still standing in front of a lovely cottage.

15 On Seneca, turn left to reach Oneida Avenue. Look for amusing details along this street. When visiting, we saw a little red teddy bear up in a tree and a weird creature contemplating a group of garden chairs.

16 Then, walk back towards the ferry on Cibola Avenue.

17 Plan some time to stop at the funky **Island Café** on your right (for great food, drinks, treats and island ambiance!).

Or, if you're in no rush, you could go to the **Rectory Café**.

Rectory Café

18 Last winter, we had brunch on a Sunday inside the cosy dining room. The summer before, we savoured cocktails and dessert on the patio (blissful moment at the end of the day). You'll find paninis and bison burgers on their menu (not cheap but we want them to stay in business, right?). The restaurant opens daily at 11 a.m.

9

10

11

11

12

13

YORKVILLE
VIP STROLL
28

The ultimate indulgence stroll

Once in a while, a gal needs to indulge in the best our city has to offer. It doesn't have to be the most expensive choices: quick stop, Italian style, in a tiny espresso bar and serious window shopping (there's **Holt Renfrew** and **Hazelton Lanes**, with Yorkville and Cumberland in between). Go for high tea at **MoRoCo** (or a small chocolate fondue if you want to show some restraint). For the big finish, you can opt for a movie in the VIP screening rooms at the **Varsity** and cocktails with spectacular view at **Panorama**, or a Parisian-like meal at **La Société Bistro** followed by drinks on the **Hyatt's Roof Lounge**. I'm sure your girlfriends will agree you all deserve it!

STROLL 28

Full loop:
2.4 km (35 min)

Shorter version:
The section of this stroll along Cumberland St. and north of it, is less than 1 km (15 min).

Game for more?
The **University of Toronto Ivy League Stroll** (**Stroll 8**, p. 49) is just west of Bloor and Avenue Road.

Parking & TTC
• Exit at **Bay Subway Station**.
• The **Green P** at 37 Yorkville (east of Bay) is cheaper than the one at 74 Yorkville.

Other TIPS
• You can get 90 minutes of free parking at **Hazelton Lanes** (entrance on Avenue Road) if you buy $25 or more at the **Whole Food** grocery store and have your parking ticket validated at the cashier.
• The **Varsity** in **Manulife Centre** includes VIP screening rooms. See **cinemaclock. com** for its listings. You'll also find a large **Indigo** in Manulife, one floor below the cinema.

Bellair Street

1 After parking in one of the two **Green P** parking lots on Yorkville Avenue, walk west, then turn south on Bellair Street. Note that **Café Nervosa**, in the pretty house at the corner of Yorkville and Bellair, has a very lovely patio on its second floor (tiny, but a great option for a late lunch).

2 See if you can find a stool at **Zaza's** perfect little Italian espresso bar (next door on Bellair). You'll be elbow to elbow with strangers but the enthusiastic staff will make you feel at home. If too crowded, simply go further down to **Lettieri**, at the corner of Bellair and Cumberland, for your coffee fix.

Bellair includes fun stores to sift through: **Rolo** is filled with funky trinkets (24 Bellair), and **Kumari's** and **Laywine's**, across the street, with a wide selection of accessories and quality gadgets.

Cumberland Street

3 Chic **Sassafraz**, with its tables by the windows at Cumberland, is a favourite spot to see and be seen.

(For the kids in your life I recommend a visit to **Kidding Awound** to your left at 91 Cumberland.)

4 Further west on Cumberland is a line-up of fashion stores to discover, including the original clothes of **Motion** (106), the high-end consignment store **L'elegante** (132), topped with edgy men's boutique **Serpentine** where samurai meets rock star.

5 Facing them all is the unique **Yorkville Park**, a patchwork of small gardens starting with a 650-ton mound of granite.

If you're not going for one of the fancier restaurant suggestions described in this stroll, you can grab a gourmet sandwich at **MBCo** (impressive and expensive) and eat it while sitting in the beautiful little park.

Or you can access the **Coffee Mill** with a courtyard at the end of the corridor to the left of the **Guild Shop** (118 Cumberland).

6 **Carole's Cheesecake Café** at 114 Cumberland is another one with lunch options under $10. (I enjoyed a piece of their decadent cheesecake while sitting at one of their cute front tables.)

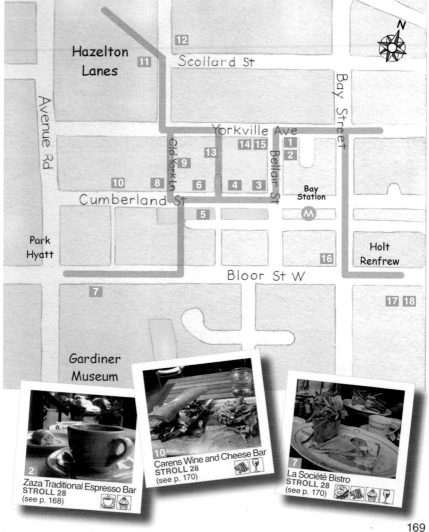

Zaza Traditional Espresso Bar
STROLL 28
(see p. 168)

Carens Wine and Cheese Bar
STROLL 28
(see p. 170)

La Société Bistro
STROLL 28
(see p. 170)

Bloor Street West

Behind the granite mound is the **Nike** store. Walk through it to reach Bloor Street (by **Winners**). Between Yonge and Avenue Road, you'll find many high-end boutiques amidst the major chains' trendy flagship stores (an occasion to see the current lines from **Prada**, **Coach** and the likes).

7 I ate the fanciest fries at **La Société Bistro**, up the stairs in 131 Bloor W.: in a cute wire basket, under a Tiffany-like ceiling. Everything we tasted in this French bistro was excellent.

Old York Lane

8 We thought the yellow canopy at **Hemingways'** (142 Cumberland), filtering the summer light, gave us all a lovely glow! On its side, a mural marks the entrance to the prettiest alley in town: Old York Lane.

9 Across the lane, **Remy's** second-floor patio serves the same kind of pub fare and drinks.

10 We had wonderful food in a secluded and stylish back patio at **Carens Wine and Cheese Bar** (158 Cumberland, west of **Hemingway's**).

Hazelton Avenue

11 At the end of the lane, cross Yorkville and continue into Hazelton, with scattered outdoor art from the galleries (see the pieces south of **Myriam Shiell Fine Art**). Pathways lead to **Hazelton Lanes**.

My favourite stores to explore within **Hazelton Lanes** are the three really cool **TNT** high-end stores.

12 We saw a fantastic choir across the street at **Heliconian Hall**. (See **heliconianclub.org** for their line of shows.)

Yorkville Avenue

Back on Hazelton Avenue, turn left on Yorkville for a visit to gorgeous lifestyle store **Teatro Verde** (98 Yorkville).

Another must-stop is the designer consignment **Second Time Around** at 99 Yorkville. It's also where you'll find **MoRoCo**, hidden from the street.

13 Its ultra feminine white shop displaying macarons and chocolates is followed by the baroque dining room. We went for their absolutely decadent **Afternoon Tea** ($50 per person, served from 2:30 p.m. to 5 p.m.) but there are less expensive options to fully enjoy the chichi experience (fancy lunch menu, teas and cocktails).

14 Another fun experience would be to get the table for four in the small alcove by the window at **Koko! Share Bar** (81 Yorkville) and try their "share plates".

15 Don't miss the whimsical duo of **Free People** (79 Yorkville) and **Anthropologie** across the street as you walk towards Bay.

Bay Street

16 Turn right on Bay Street for serious shoe stores: **Specchio** (1240 Bay), **Davids** and **Capezio** at the corner of Bay and Bloor. Then head east to **Holt Renfrew** (with four floors of high-end designer clothing.

At the mezzanine level is the slick and fancy **Holt's Café**, with a long expressionist painting facing the wall of bay windows. At the concourse level (where you'll find **Holt Gourmet**, a trendy cafeteria-style space) you can follow the underground corridor to reach the **Manulife Centre** and the **Varsity Cinemas**.

The big finish

17 For a decent extra fee, the **Varsity** offers small VIP screening rooms (they're licensed, have oversized seating and staff to take concession orders).

18 After your movie, take the elevator by the cinema to get to aptly named **Panorama**, on the 51st floor of the **Manulife Centre**, for tapas-like entrées and drinks. See what kind of view a $13 cocktail gets you! (19-years +, expect small cover charge on Fridays and Saturdays.)

You might be tempted instead to visit the **Roof Lounge** on the 18th floor of the **Park Hyatt** (at 4 Avenue Rd.) to have a drink while admiring the city on their small year-round outdoor patio.

To mark a special occasion, there's the gorgeous and soothing **Stillwater Spa** in the lower floor of the hotel.

Their treatments are expensive but it's quite something to walk through a corridor of glass tiles with water gently running under your feet as you reach the elegant tea lounge with the calming effect of fish tanks.

SUGGESTION INDEX

Do you need a caffeine fix?
Are you hungry for breakfast?
Do you want to have lunch?
Do you deserve a treat?
How about an afternoon drink?

Do you want to find a stroll around a good place
for your caffeine fix?

Second Cup
STROLL 1
(see p. 18)

Dark Horse Espresso Bar
STROLL 4
(see p. 33)

Balzac's Coffee Roasters
STROLL 7
(see p. 44)

Best urban patio!
Overlooking Royal York Hotel.
Open Monday to Saturday 8 a.m,
9:30 a.m. on Sundays.

Huge café in Chinatown
Fantastic coffee, great decor.
Open weekdays at 7 a.m. and
at 8 a.m. on weekends.

In historic Distillery District
Beautiful building with mezzanine.
Open Monday to Saturday at 7
a.m. and at 8 a.m. on Sundays.

b Espresso Bar
STROLL 8
(see p. 50)

Café Belong (Grab & Go)
STROLL 12
(see p. 76)

Boulangerie Cocoa
STROLL 14
(see p. 88)

In superb Royal Conservatory
Excellent treats and light meals.
Open weekdays at 8 a.m., Sat-
urday 9 a.m., Sunday 11 a.m.

In Evergreen Brick Works
Take-out counter with great coffee.
Open 8 a.m. to 5 p.m. (opens at 9
a.m. on Sundays).

By Etobicoke's waterfront
Starbucks coffee, great crêpes.
Open weekdays at 7 a.m., Satur-
day 7:30 a.m, Sunday 8:30 a.m.

Jet Fuel Coffee Shop
STROLL 15
(see p. 96)

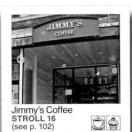

Jimmy's Coffee
STROLL 16
(see p. 102)

Atelier Café Lounge
STROLL 18
(see p. 113)

In historic Cabbagetown
Serious coffee, foamiest lattes.
Open daily at 7 a.m. (great morn-
ing treats sold out by 11 a.m.).

In funky Kensington Market
*Long, narrow, amazing patio
with trees!*
Open daily from 7 a.m. to 8 p.m.

Exotic lounge on King Street
Coffee, light fare... and cushions.
Open weekdays from 8:30 a.m.
to 6 p.m.

"Many coffee shops can fix great chai lattes
for tea lovers."

Sense Appeal Coffee Roasters
STROLL 18
(see p. 114)

Te Aro
STROLL 19
(see p. 118)

Balzac's Coffee Roasters
STROLL 20
(see p. 126)

Upstairs at Spadina & Adelaide
Excellent coffee, tasty treats.
Open weekdays at 7:30 a.m.,
weekends at 9 a.m.

In a Leslieville converted garage
Roasted on site, yummy treats.
Open weekdays 7 a.m., Saturday 7:30 a.m., Sunday 8 a.m.

In heart of Liberty Village
Fabulous tile flooring!
Open weekdays at 7 a.m., Saturday 8 a.m., Sunday 9 a.m.

Capital Espresso
STROLL 21
(see p. 131)

Rooster Coffee House
STROLL 22
(see p. 137)

Merchants of Green Coffee
STROLL 23
(see p. 140)

Exposed-brick café in Parkdale
Excellent lattes, yummy muffins.
Open weekdays at 7 a.m. and
at 8 a.m. on weekends.

Facing great Riverdale Park
So inviting, great coffee and treats.
Open daily from 7 a.m. to 7
p.m.

Off the beaten track Riverside
Large cosy place all about coffee.
Open weekdays at 8 a.m. and
at 10 a.m. on weekends.

Dark Horse Espresso Bar
STROLL 23
(see p. 142)

Dark Horse Espresso Bar
STROLL 26
(see p. 158)

Zaza Traditional Espresso Bar
STROLL 28
(see p. 168)

Communal table in Riverside
Fantastic coffee, great treats.
Open daily at 7 a.m. (outside
benches to catch the sun).

Their newest on Queen West
Great decor! Same super coffee.
Open weekdays at 7 a.m. and
at 8 a.m. on weekends.

Dolce vita in posh Yorkville
Tiniest and cutest Italian café.
Open Monday to Saturday at 8
a.m., Sunday at 10 a.m.

"All the restaurants serve coffee but it's not always memorable. These coffee shops will do the trick."

Do you want to find a stroll around a good place
for decadent treats?

Petit Four Bakery
STROLL 1
(see p. 16)

Café Crêpe
STROLL 4
(see p. 32)

Brick Street Bakery
STROLL 7
(see p. 46)

Financial district's sweet side
All kinds of goodies for take out.
Open weekdays 7:30 a.m. to 8
p.m. (closes at 3 p.m. on Fridays).

A bit of Paris on Queen West
All sorts of sweet and salty crêpes.
Open weekdays at 8:30 a.m.,
weekends at 9 a.m.

Cute patio at The Distillery
Decadent sausage rolls.
Open daily at 8:30 a.m. (you can
eat your take out on their patio).

Phipps Bakery Café
STROLL 10
(see p. 66)

Brioche Dorée
STROLL 18
(see p. 111)

Soma Chocolatemaker
STROLL 18
(see p. 114)

Scrumptious Eglinton West
Cakes, cookies, squares...
Open Monday to Saturday at 8:30
a.m., Sundays at 10 a.m.

Just east of Bathurst
Vast choice, airy space.
Open at 7 a.m. on weekdays
and 8 a.m. on weekends.

Artisan chocolate on King
Eat treat in beautiful back store.
Open weekdays 9 a.m., Saturday
12 noon (closed on Sundays).

Ed's Real Scoop
STROLL 19
(see p. 116)

Bobbette & Belle
STROLL 19
(see p. 118)

Ambiance Chocolat
STROLL 23
(see p. 142)

Leslieville's yummy gelato
Blueberry pie, cinnamon, ginger...
Open daily at 11:30 a.m.
(specials on pints in the winter)

Leslieville's prettiest parlour
*Exquisite macarons, cupcakes
and scones with fresh cream.*
Open daily from 9 a.m.

Riverside's sweet secret
Amazing artisanal chocolate.
Open weekdays 10 a.m., Saturday
11 a.m, Sunday 12 noon.

"Spread the joy. Bring some to your loved ones!"

Desmond & Beatrice
STROLL 23
(see p. 142)

Chocolate by Wickerhead
STROLL 25
(see p. 150)

Remarkable Bean
STROLL 25
(see p. 150)

Cute as a button on Queen East
Colourful cupcakes and more.
Open 10 a.m. to 7 p.m. Tuesday
to Sunday (closed on Mondays).

Best chocolate at The Beach
Great look, taste and prices.
Closed Mondays, open weekdays
at 1 p.m on, weekends at 11 a.m.

Best salty muffins at The Beach
Savory and cream cheese? Yum!
Great coffee too. Open daily
from 7 a.m. to 10 p.m.

The Pie Shack
STROLL 25
(see p. 152)

Dufflet
STROLL 25
(see p. 154)

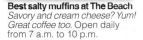

Red Tea Box
STROLL 26
(see p. 158)

Country feel at The Beach
Huge pie slices, they supply
boardgames and books.
Open daily from 11 a.m.

Prettiest Dufflet is in The Beach
Check their back store!
Open weekday at 9 a.m., Satur-
day 10 a.m., Sunday 11 a.m.

Whimsical in Trinity-Bellwoods
Cakes too cute to eat, special teas.
Closed on Tuesdays, open daily at
10 a.m. (Sunday at 12 noon).

Nadège Patisserie
STROLL 26
(see p. 159)

Carole's Cheesecake Café
STROLL 28
(see p. 169)

MoRoCo Chocolat
STROLL 28
(see p. 171)

Gem by Trinity-Bellwoods Park
Beautifully crafted pastries
(also croissant and macarons
experts). Open daily at 8 a.m.

Let's get cheesy in Yorkville
All sorts of cheesecakes, all-day
breakfast and more. Open daily at
10 a.m. (closed on Sundays).

Afternoon tea in Yorkville
Finger sandwiches, tea... Served
weekdays from 10 a.m., weekends
from 12 noon (closed Mondays).

"Many decadent shops do not offer seating."

Do you want to find a stroll around a good place
for breakfast?

Cora's
STROLL 3
(see p. 24)

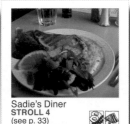

Sadie's Diner
STROLL 4
(see p. 33)

Hank's
STROLL 7
(see p. 48)

Colourful start at Wellington
Great presentation, large portions.
Open daily 6 a.m. to 3 p.m.
(opens at 7 a.m. on Sundays).

Diner with a twist at Portland
Funky and pretty, great food
Open weekdays at 7:30 a.m.
and 9 a.m. on weekends.

Near the Flatiron Building
Great food, served with a smile.
Open weekdays 7 a.m. to 4
p.m. (8 a.m. on weekends).

L'Espresso Bar Mercurio
STROLL 8
(see p. 50)

Eggspectation
STROLL 9
(see p. 60)

Hotel Gelato
STROLL 10
(see p. 64)

On Bloor West, by U of T
Very classy, very good. Open
weekdays at 7:30 a.m., weekends
9 a.m. (brunch starts at 10 a.m.).

By the Eaton Centre
Huge menu, cool space.
Open daily at 7 a.m. (they also
have a lunch menu).

Glam café on Eglinton West
Quality food and presentation.
Open daily at 8 a.m. (they also
have lunch and dinner menus).

Boulangerie Cocoa
STROLL 14
(see p. 88)

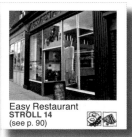

Easy Restaurant
STROLL 14
(see p. 90)

Johnny G.
STROLL 15
(see p. 95)

By Etobicoke's waterfront
Starbucks coffee, great crêpes.
Open weekdays at 7 a.m., Satur-
day 7:30 a.m., Sunday 8:30 a.m.

At the foot of Roncesvalles
*All-day breakfast and lunch (check
their retro sign on King!).*
Open daily from 9 a.m. to 5 p.m.

Greasy spoon in Cabbagetown
Easy going staff, good portions.
Open weekdays at 7:30 a.m.
and at 8:30 a.m. on weekends.

"When a muffin or a scone won't do."

Morning Glory
STROLL 17
(see p. 104)

Le Petit Déjeuner
STROLL 17
(see p. 107)

Lady Marmalade
STROLL 19
(see p. 116)

Cute little thing in Corktown
All-day breakfast. Closed Tuesday and Wednesday. Open weekdays 8:30 a.m., weekends 9 a.m.

"C'est très bon" on King
Cool booths, original breakfasts. Open weekdays at 8 a.m., weekends 9 a.m.

Leslieville's most popular Lady
Tasty, fresh and plentiful. Open daily at 8 a.m. (they also have a lunch menu, cash only)

School Bakery
STROLL 20
(see p. 126)

Mitzy's Café
STROLL 21
(see p. 128)

Bonjour Brioche Bakery Café
STROLL 23
(see p. 140)

Back to School at Liberty
Cool dark room, original menu. Open weekdays at 8 a.m. and at 9:30 a.m. on weekends.

Off Queen West
Cottage-like, cosy, yummy... Open weekdays at 7:30 a.m. and at 9 a.m. on weekends.

"Ze real ting" in Riverside
Perfect traditional French bakery. Closed on Mondays, open other days from 8 a.m. to 4 p.m.

Juice and Java
STROLL 25
(see p. 152)

Gladstone Café
STROLL 26
(see p. 160)

Carole's Cheesecake Café
STROLL 28
(see p. 169)

The crêpe place at The Beach
Large restaurant, all kinds of crêpes. Open weekdays at 7 a.m., Saturday at 8 a.m., Sunday at 9 a.m.

In historic Gladstone Hotel
Fresh food, lovely building with gallery on each floor. Open daily at 7 a.m.

A few steps down in Yorkville
Full breakfast and lunch menu, and cheesecakes! Open daily at 10 a.m. (closed on Sundays).

"Most restaurants listed in this guide also offer a brunch menu on the weekends."

Do you want to find a stroll around a great place
for a casual lunch?

O & B Canteen
STROLL 1
(see p. 14)

Perfect combo with TIFF movie
Everything is delicious in this lovely urban setting!
Open daily at 8 a.m.

Marché Restaurant
STROLL 1
(see p. 16)

Indoor patio under the arches
Fun concept with food stations to explore all day long
Open daily at 6:30 a.m.

Queen Mother Café
STROLL 4
(see p. 32)

Timeless on Queen West
Amazing "pan-global" affordable menu (many vegetarian options)
Open daily at 11:30 a.m.

Java House
STROLL 4
(see p. 33)

Truly funky Queen West
Doesn't get better for the price!
Open weekdays at 9 a.m. and at 8 a.m. on weekends.

Shanghai Cowgirl
STROLL 4
(see p. 34)

Cool greasy spoon place
Very good, with booths and fun art on the wall (great patio)
Open daily at 11:30 a.m.

Phipps Bakery
STROLL 10
(see p. 66)

Comfort food on Eglinton West
Best mac and cheese, soups...
Open Monday to Saturday at 8:30 a.m. and at 10 a.m. on Sundays.

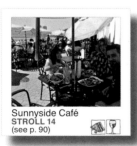

Sunnyside Café
STROLL 14
(see p. 90)

Lunch by the boardwalk
Decent food, fantastic view
Open daily at around 11:30 a.m.
(seasonal, call 416-531-1122).

The Grilled Cheese
STROLL 16
(see p. 98)

Perfect Kensington feel
Excellent grilled cheese... (what else?)
Open daily at 11 a.m.

Le Ti Colibri
STROLL 16
(see p. 100)

French Caribbean Kensington
Appetizing creole food, exotic patio in the back. Open daily at 12 noon.

"Think good old carbs! But there are other options too..."

Waterfalls Indian Tapas
STROLL 16
(see p. 100)

Sharing food in Kensington
Excellent food, pretty cocktails, fun patio along Augusta. Open daily from 11:30 a.m.

Gilead Café
STROLL 17
(see p. 104)

Hidden treasure in Corktown
Airy little space serving tasty food. Open Monday to Saturday 8 a.m. to 3 p.m., Sundays 10 a.m. to 3 p.m.

The One That Got Away
STROLL 18
(see p. 113)

Unassuming on trendy King
Everything fish, all kinds of fish Open weekdays at 11 a.m., weekends at 12 noon.

Hanoi 3 Seasons
STROLL 19
(see p. 119)

North Vietnam in Leslieville
Delicious, affordable. Tuesday to Sunday, 12 noon to 3 p.m.; reopens at 5 p.m. (cash only)

Poor John's Café
STROLL 21
(see p. 128)

Rich idea on Queen West
Superb sandwiches! Open Monday to Saturday at 9 a.m. and at 10 a.m. on Sundays.

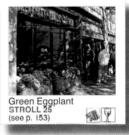

Green Eggplant
STROLL 25
(see p. 153)

Sure value in The Beach
Colourful, reliable food, cocktails... Open Monday to Friday at 11 a.m. and at 9 a.m. on weekends.

Lion on the Beach
STROLL 25
(see p. 154)

Cool patio on Queen East
Best way to enjoy a sunny day at The Beach. Open daily from 11:30 a.m.

Drake's Corner Café
STROLL 26
(see p. 160)

Funky chic on Queen West
Fun decor, great food and garage door open onto the patio Open daily at 8 a.m.

MBCo
STROLL 28
(see p. 169)

Great take out in Yorkville
Eat in the restaurant or grab a decadent sandwich to eat in the park! Open daily at 8 a.m.

Note that we don't have a symbol for dinner, only lunch.
"Many of these also offer a dinner menu, call to confirm."

Do you want to find a stroll around a good place
for a fancy lunch?

Pearl Harbourfront
STROLL 6
(see p. 40)

Large waterfront windows
You select dim sum from a cart.
Open weekdays at 11 a.m. and
at 10:30 a.m. on weekends.

L'Espresso Bar Mercurio
STROLL 8
(see p. 50)

Classy by the university
Airy with high ceilings, tasty food.
Open weekdays at 8 a.m., 9 a.m.
on weekends (brunch starts at 10)

Bannock
STROLL 11
(see p. 71)

New at Queen West & Bay
Original, best fancy poutine.
Dining room open daily 11:30
a.m. (Sundays, open at 11 a.m.)

Café Belong
STROLL 12
(see p. 76)

In Evergreen Brick Works
Fancy food in industrial decor.
Open weekdays from 11:30 a.m.,
weekends from 11 a.m.

Brassaii
STROLL 18
(see p. 113)

Hidden courtyard off King
*Gorgeous inside out, original
food.* Open daily at least from
10:30 a.m.

Mildred's Temple Kitchen
STROLL 20
(see p. 124)

Chill out in Liberty Village
Beautiful decor, colourful menu.
Open weekdays at 11:45 a.m.
and at 10 a.m. on weekends.

Carens Wine and Cheese Bar
STROLL 28
(see p. 170)

Hidden backyard in Yorkville
Delicious food, best backyard!
Opens daily at 11:30 a.m.
(near **Cumberland Cinema**!)

Holt's Café
STROLL 28
(see p. 172)

In mezzanine at Holt Renfrew
Beautiful modern decor.
Open from 10 a.m. Monday to
Saturday, Sundays at 12 noon.

La Société Bistro
STROLL 28
(see p. 170)

Upstairs on Bloor West
French bistro experience.
Open weekdays from 11:30 a.m.,
weekends from 11 a.m.

Note that some restaurants close after lunch to get set up for dinner.
"For ladies who lunch (it's cheaper than dinner)."

Do you want to find a stroll around a good place
for late afternoon drinks?

Against the Grain
STROLL 5
(see p. 36)

By Lake Ontario
Large waterfront patio.
Open weekdays at 11 a.m. and at 10:30 a.m. on weekends.

Martini Bar
STROLL 9
(see p. 60)

In a boutique hotel on Victoria
Good martinis and fries!
They offer $6 martinis everyday from 4 p.m. to 6 p.m.

Dogfish Pub
STROLL 13
(see p. 83)

By Bluffer's Park Marina
View of the Bluffs and marina.
Open daily at 11 a.m. (but seasonal, call 416-264-2337).

Pacific Junction Hotel
STROLL 17
(see p. 106)

On King East
Utterly funky bar, fun menu.
Weekdays from 12 noon, Saturday 5 p.m., closed Sundays.

Joy Bistro Bar
STROLL 19
(see p. 116)

Patio facing Leslieville park
Two patios, happy hour.
Open weekdays at 11 a.m. and at 8 a.m. on weekends.

Goods & Provisions
STROLL 19
(see p. 118)

Cocktail hour in Leslieville
Perfect food to accompany drinks. Open daily from 5:30 p.m. (closed on Sundays).

Allen's
STROLL 22
(see p. 137)

On Danforth near Broadview
Backyard patio with mature trees.
Open weekdays at 11:30 a.m. and at 10:30 a.m. on weekends.

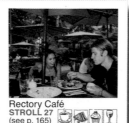

Rectory Café
STROLL 27
(see p. 165)

On Ward's Island
Perfect patio, cosy indoors.
Open daily at 11 a.m. (closed Monday & Tuesday after mid-October)

Hemingway's
STROLL 28
(see p. 170)

Laid-back in chic Yorkville
Second floor patio under canopy, overlooking Old York Lane.
Open daily from 11 a.m. to 2 p.m.

Note that many places stretch the patio season with heaters.
"Nothing feels like a holiday like having a drink on a patio!"

ALPHABETICAL INDEX

ALPHABETICAL INDEX

ALPAHBETICAL INDEX

ALPHABETICAL INDEX

ALPAHBETICAL INDEX

ALPHABETICAL INDEX

Make this **combo**
work for you!

Leave **Toronto Fun Places** with your family while you take off for a few hours to enjoy Toronto with your girlfriends, **Toronto Urban Strolls** in hand. Everybody wins!

Sold in the **Travel** section of major bookstores, or online at: **www.torontofunplaces.com**

Because **happy mom = happy family**
(or is it the other way around?)